MW00938547

"John Perkins' combat methods [Guided Chaos] are the most efficient and devastating that I have experienced before, during, and since the military."
–Ret. Lieutenant Dick Shea, original Navy SEAL team member

"John Perkins is an expert on the dynamics of violence."
–Dr. Peter Pizzola, Director, NYPD Crime Lab

"I've used John Perkins' methods myself in the street, and they really work"
–Jim Cirillo, Top Member NYPD Stakeout Squad

"Your book 'Attackproof' and the 'Attackproof Companion DVD Series' stand unparalleled in the annals of self-defense and security training."
–Charl Viljoen, Regional Director of the Guardian Angels, Capetown South Africa "The Most Violent City in the World"

"I am the Element Leader of our Tactical Team and a Defensive Tactics Instructor. I have been a Police Officer for 18 years. I have been to many schools, classes and seminars throughout my career in the Marine Corps and in law enforcement…The training we have received from John Perkins has profoundly influenced the way our operators and instructors train and teach."
–Detective Michael Goldman, NYS Police Defensive Tactics Instructor

"Grand Master Perkins is, in my humble opinion, the most unique figure in the world of Combat, Combatives and Surviving violent encounters. Grand Master Perkins is unlike anyone I have ever met, trained with, know about, have read about or that I have even heard about. He has fused physical, basic combative techniques with forensic knowledge and principles to create the most unique, effective and complete combat system in existence today."
–The Honorable RJB, Former Acting Supreme Court Justice in the State of New York

"Real World Violence, not Dojo Dancing. I have trained, studied, and researched martial arts and fighting for over twenty-five years and have always felt that something was missing. The number of techniques I found to actually work in a real fight was very few, even though I became very proficient at utilizing them in the dojo…if you do have a martial arts background you'll find that many of the things you will learn…will greatly enhance what you know already."
–David Chesher, Former SWAT team member and U.S. Marine

"[John Perkins] Changed the Way I Train and Think About Self-Defense."
–Bob Miller, Corrections Officer, Oregon

"The other martial arts are about beautiful choreography. There's nothing dance-like about this."
–Eric Haney, Command Sergeant Major (retired) founding member Delta Force from SPYMASTER on The Learning Channel

"I've been in hundreds of street fights. And I teach JKD and I can honestly tell you what John Perkins teaches is the best stuff out there for street fighting.
–Mike Muratore, JKD instructor Los Angeles, CA under Jerry Poteet (original Bruce Lee student)

"John Perkins is America's Foremost Self Protection Expert."
–Gerald Celente, Trends Research Institute, the World's #1 Trends Forecaster

"I unreservedly endorse John Perkins' programs."
–Bradley J. Steiner, President, International Combat Martial Arts Federation

"The difference between boxing and street fights is that many street fights can mean life or death. John Perkins teaches the most effective and easy to learn methods of self-defense in existence today."
–Doug Gray, Former Super Welterweight Champion of the NABO

"The Kill the Enemy DVD is the greatest work of modern combat of our time. In the dirty bloody world of real combat there are no second place winners. In combat there is only kill and come home. John trains you for just such an encounter…he has found a way to bridge the gap between school and real world, no-holds-barred REALITY."
–Captain Jonathan Edwards, U.S. Army Ranger 101st Airborne/Air Assault

"As a marine I've trained all over the world in most of the major hand-to-hand systems. When I first heard about John Perkins' system, I was skeptical. After touching hands with him, I instantly knew this was like nothing I had ever experienced before or during my military career. I also knew I would someday have to master it."
–Lt. Col Al Ridenhour USMC, Instructor in Unarmed Combat in Iraq; Guided Chaos /Guided Chaos Combatives Master

From www.attackproof.com:

HOW TO FIGHT FOR YOUR LIFE:

ENHANCED REALITY-BASED CLOSE COMBAT TRAINING FOR SELF DEFENSE AND STREET SURVIVAL

John Perkins, Grand Master
Al Ridenhour, 7th degree Master
Matt Kovsky, 6th degree Master

Adaptive Defense Inc.
Attack Proof Inc.
Mad Squirrel Productions Inc.

New York, USA

COPYRIGHT WARNING

This publication is protected under the US Copyright Act of 1976 and all other applicable international, federal, state and local laws, and all rights are reserved, including resale rights.

By law: It is illegal to give or sell this Guide to anyone else. If you received this publication from anyone other than attackproof.com, it is a pirated copy. Please notify us at: attackproof@mail.websitewizard.com   Thank you.

This publication contains Trade and Service-marked names protected by U.S. Trademark laws.

Copyright © by
Grand Master John Perkins,
Master Al Ridenhour 7th degree,
Master Matt Kovsky 6th degree

Adaptive Defense Inc.
Attack Proof Inc.
Mad Squirrel Productions Inc.

All Rights Reserved

Special thanks to Ari Kandel, 3rd degree and Patrick Jones, 2nd degree, for their assistance in proofreading and editing this manual. Thanks also to Master Michael Watson, 4th degrees Joseph Troy and Joe Martarano, 3rd degree Andre Deveaux and Jeanine Paolo, 1st degree, for modeling the photos in this manual.

GCC logo and cover designed by Joseph Troy.

Go to www.attackproof.com and www.guidedchaoscombatives.com where you can find DVDs, video downloads as well as a forum and blog where you can ask questions and learn a tremendous amount from the most congenial martial artists on the web.

WARNING

The skills and techniques in this manual are for self-defense purposes only and are inherently dangerous. It is best to avoid violence in any way possible unless your life or a loved one's is in peril.

Use caution when practicing these techniques. Use eye protection when working with partners. Consult a physician to determine if you are healthy enough to engage in such activities. Since we cannot be with you when you train, we cannot be responsible for the improper use or practice of the methods described herein.

NOTE: Ideal training tools for practicing Guided Chaos Combatives solo are Muay Thai heavy bags (5-6 feet tall for practicing low kicks and minimizing swing) and so called "Body Opponent Bags" or BOBs which are rubberized dummies simulating a human torso. Both are available on line in martial arts supply stores. Get the "deluxe" extended BOB model for practicing groin strikes using the hands and knees.

TABLE OF CONTENTS

INTRODUCTION

> **UGLY TRUTHS:**
> 1. When you have *seconds* to live, help is only *minutes* away.
> 2. Assume no one is coming to save you.

This reference manual serves as a guide to some of the key concepts and drills contained within Guided Chaos Combatives. These easy-to-learn skills are culled from military close combat and are a refinement of training *previously* taught to U.S. Soldiers and Marines dating back to WWII (before the training became "politically correct" and influenced by sport-fighting). They were and are a combat-proven, lethal, life and death fighting methodology. Most of it can be practiced solo, but having training partners is ideal.

This course of instruction is applicable for people of all fitness levels and is not limited to military and law enforcement personnel. There are no controlling or sportive techniques taught; GCC was created to provide *ordinary* people with the necessary skills to *swiftly* take out an attacker. The GCC methodology is NOT designed for sport or competitive fighting.

We must state clearly at the outset that you should avoid violence at all costs except to save your life or a loved one's. Beyond this, NO fight is worth it. Even if you legitimately defended yourself, a jury could decide otherwise and you could find yourself in prison for a very long time. At the end of this manual we give you legal tips to help avoid this scenario. But understand that GCC is dramatically effective in 90% of the actual assaults or attacks a *normal, levelheaded, law-abiding citizen* might encounter. That does NOT include the kind of moronic, ego-based, alcohol or drug-fueled throw-downs that are easily avoided using the material in this manual. If *that* is your interest, and you're looking for "secrets" that'll help you win your next cockfight, you've come to the wrong place. If you find yourself getting sucked into bar fights, pissing contests, challenge matches or the public, social or domestic dramas of your emotionally disturbed "friends" or family with any kind of frequency, it's time for a Reality Check—otherwise your wake up call may be in a cell, hospital or morgue.

What is Guided Chaos *Combatives*?
It Is the First Part of Guided Chaos...

Guided Chaos is an esoteric, advanced and *adaptive* self-defense system invented by former forensic crime scene expert John Perkins in 1978. It is completely unique, stunningly effective and takes many years to master. However, the *first part* of Guided Chaos, called Guided Chaos Combatives, is remarkably simple. It is a self-contained system comprised of basic World War II era strikes and strategies that were designed to be taught to our troops in mere *hours* before shipping out for jungle warfare in the Pacific against the Japanese, who were all assumed to be karate and judo experts. John Perkins, who is a certified Grandmaster in Combat Martial Arts under the International Combat Martial Arts Federation, has modified and improved these techniques by imbuing them with some of the far more advanced motion principles of Guided Chaos, the most important of which being Dropping Energy. GCC is extremely easy to learn and practice on your own.

The relevance and context of GCC to Guided Chaos can be found in ATTACK PROOF, 2ND EDITION. Especially useful for the study of GCC and developing a "warrior's mindset" is the "SURVIVAL MANIFESTO" starting on page 247 of ATTACK PROOF, however the essence of it is contained in this manual.

I. AWARENESS

> Awareness is one of the most ignored concepts of most martial arts training; yet it is one of the most important aspects of self-defense. Understand that Awareness is not paranoia but rather simply developing the habit of present moment awareness when out in public. It is remarkably easy in today's culture to become lost inside your iPod or Blackberry, mindlessly texting or tweeting while predators prepare to pounce. These are just a few examples of what we're going to discuss to save your life.

Take the Awareness Test

Humans are creatures of habit and once we've established certain behavior patterns it can be hard to break them. When it comes to awareness, these established patterns could become dangerous. Today's techno culture encourages separation from your environment and the things and people in it by focusing your mind on iPods, iPhones, as well as your inner dialogue concerning appointments, past and future conversations, day-dreaming-- virtually everything *except* what's going on around you. Predators depend on this, which is why pickpockets at the least and serial killers at the worst seem to appear "out of nowhere" to rob, kidnap, assault, rape or kill the oblivious pedestrian.

What NOT to do! Be aware of your environment when out in public! Texting and Tweeting makes you a sitting duck...

We want to be clear here that we're not talking about an *assassination-*style attack where you are stealthily stalked and executed. Despite what movies depict, there is no self-defense against assassination, unless you have a cadre of secret service personnel, and even *then* it's doubtful. The goal of most street attacks is intimidation, wanton violence, robbery, rape and abduction and most often they're executed with far less sophistication than a planned "hit." Murder, however may become a byproduct of any of these. Here, Awareness plays the primary role in your survival and you don't want to do anything faddish, ignorant or narcissistic to impair it.

Our primitive awareness instincts that *used* to alert our ancestors to danger as far ahead in time and space as possible are not only muted nowadays but also *distorted,* as we'll explain below. If you were walking down some city street and turned a corner to see a gang of surly teenagers hanging out on a loading dock some seventy feet away, what would you do?

- If you were oblivious and involved with your own inner thoughts

14

or texting your friends you might not even see them until you were right on top of them.

- If you did see them and they gave you a funny feeling in your gut, would you attribute it to something you ate and ignore it?

- Would you acknowledge the gut feeling but squelch it because of assertiveness training? After all, you're a *strong* person (even if you're small physically) and have every right to walk where you want and they'll *respect* you for it! If you've had *sportive* MMA training, maybe you think you can "submit" one of them and the rest will quake with fear and just *watch* or run away and hide!

- Or maybe you're "highly evolved" and see all mankind as brothers that empathize with those who are different or less fortunate. They'll *acknowledge* your acceptance and compassion and return the sentiment!

- Or maybe you've been fed a diet of violent television and movies or perhaps even trained in a mass-marketed self defense system and choose to walk on the other side of the street while confidently reaching for your concealed mace, knife, handgun or mentally preparing to deliver a killer kung fu strike.

- Or maybe you're in a big rush and it's *really important* that you take the shortest route between points A and B so perhaps they'll ignore you because of your brisk pace and disinterested demeanor.

Which of these is the best response?

None of them. Your gut instinct is a gift given to all humans and even though it's screaming at you, its simple message is almost universally ignored: *"Walk down a different street!"*
It's simple: **Don't go there in the first place.** Turn around and go another way. Nobody's going to pin a medal on you for bravery if you're already dead.

Simple Everyday Awareness Strategies

> The following tips provide some specific street smarts applicable to everyday life. The common theme is understanding that although we don't live in a war zone, we also shouldn't live in "La-La land." Being aware of the danger potential in each scenario allows for simple precautions that can prevent crime from happening to you in the first place. Then you won't *have* to fight, which is always the best option.

Being Aware at Automated Teller Machines (ATMs)

ATMs, especially in isolated areas at night, are frequently crime scenes. Not just robberies, but also assaults, abductions, rapes and murders often begin at ATMs. Visit ATMs only in busy, populated areas and during the day. Here are a few other tips:

1) Check out the surrounding area before approaching the ATM
2) At a drive-up ATM, don't park your car as you execute your transaction. Keep it in Drive with your foot on the brake, doors locked, ready to hit the gas at the first sign of trouble. Don't allow yourself to get boxed in by other cars.
3) Don't keep a regular ATM schedule. Vary the times and locations at which you get cash. Many criminals stalk potential victims and study their habits.

Travel Tips

Like ATMs, hotels and motels are ripe hunting grounds for criminals. Be alert and stay safe while traveling.

1) **Don't allow anyone unexpected into your room.** Criminals frequently impersonate hotel staff, repair men, etc. to gain access to victims' rooms. When in doubt, call down to the front desk to confirm a knocker's identity.
2) Use a portable electronic door alarm on your hotel room door.
3) Keep valuables in the hotel safe.
4) If you return to your room and suspect that someone has entered or tampered with the door, have hotel staff check the room before you enter.

5) Stay in your room while it is being cleaned.

6) When you are out, leave a "Do Not Disturb" sign on the door and keep the radio or TV on so that it is audible through the door.

7) If you receive a phone call in your room, be sure you know exactly who is calling before giving out any information. If the caller says he is calling from the front desk or room service, hang up and call back the front desk or room service to be safe.

8) If you are out partying, whether in your hometown or abroad, stay sober and keep an eye on your drink lest drugs be slipped into it while you're not looking. Do not go to an isolated location with a new acquaintance or bring him or her back to your room.

9) Do not give out personal information to taxi drivers, hotel employees, etc.

ADDITIONAL AWARENESS TIPS:

1) **Parking lots, especially at shopping malls and convenience stores, are commonly "Crime Scene #1" in robberies, abductions, rapes and murders.** Be alert when parking as well as when you return to your car. Check out the area before parking, and again before exiting your car. Park in well-lit areas, as close to the store or security post as possible. Lock your doors and don't leave valuables or information in the car visible through the windows. When you return to your car, scan the area before approaching, and if anything seems fishy, go back to the store and get a security guard escort or call the police to check it out. Trust your instincts! Have your keys ready as you approach your car, and once inside, lock the doors immediately.

2) **On the road, never stop and pull over in a questionable area for any reason.** If you need horrific proof of this, read the "Don't Let This Happen To You" homicide stories on Attackproof.com. If you get a flat tire or another motorist signals that you have a problem with your car, keep driving until you get to a secure or populated location where you can safely check things out. A ruined rim is less valuable than your life. Likewise, if you're involved in a minor accident and your car can still move, stay in your car and signal to the other driver that you want to proceed to another location before exchanging information, and drive until you reach a populated or secure area. In traffic, try to always leave enough space around your car to allow evasive maneuvering or at least a

hard ram of the car in front of you in case of a carjacking attempt or other attack. Keep doors and windows locked whenever you are in the car to thwart carjackings or worse. Keep your gas tank more than half-full and refuel only in safe, populated areas during the day. As with any destination, look around the gas station and store for any signs of trouble before pulling up to the pumps.

3) If criminals manage to breach the doors or windows before you can hit the gas, leave the key and any valuables, bail out of the car immediately and run away. Drill with your family so that all passengers know to do this when danger strikes.

4) If you end up trapped in a car with abductors, even if they have weapons, don't allow them to take you where they want. *Crash the car.* Once the car has picked up some speed, attack the driver ferociously, gouging out his eyes and making him lose control of the wheel. Twist the wheel hard to force a crash. Don't try to get fancy with the key or gear shift. You must incapacitate the driver as quickly as possible to make him lose all control of the car. Read the "Live To Tell" and "Don't Let This Happen To You" pages on attackproof.com for real life consequences of failing to heed these tips. The lesson from these homicides: if someone offers you a ride and you decline, run your ass off if they ask twice or they turn the car around after first driving off!

5) Always keep your cell phone charged and keep a charger and spare battery in your car. If your car stops running and you're forced to pull over in an isolated location, call the police and AAA immediately and stay in the car with the doors and windows locked. Do not accept help from or open your door or window to anyone else; just waive them along.

6) **The instant you catch a glimpse of a weapon (knife, gun, bat, etc.), assuming it is not yet touching you and you are not yet restrained, RUN (or hit the gas)!** Don't wait to figure out the attacker's intentions or to hear what he has to say. Just ESCAPE, preferably towards the nearest hard cover (e.g. cars, buildings, etc.). The odds of his shooting at or pursuing you are low, as these actions would attract a lot of attention. You'll be surprised how quickly you can run when fueled by the Fight or Flight Response. Even if you're shot at, your odds of getting hit, much less in a lethal area, drop to single digits beyond a few yards' distance. It's almost impossible to effectively stab or bludgeon a person in mid-pursuit without first tackling him, and any object held in the hand

18

will slow down a person's foot speed. Don't try to zig-zag or crouch or do anything fancy. Just get behind the nearest available cover as quickly as possible, then keep running without looking back until you're in a safer place (e.g. a store or densely populated public area). KNIFE/GUN → RUN!!!

Beware Fake Police

Many predators have discovered that an easy way to quickly gain a victim's trust and compliance is to pose as a police officer or some other person of authority. The ruse can range from flashing a phony ID to authentic-looking uniforms and dashboard and roof lights on a car. It is highly unlikely, however, for a predator to have access to a uniform patrol car or officers at headquarters who will vouch for him. These are the giveaways you can use to confirm a suspect officer's identity if you ever get into any of the following situations:

1) It is uncommon for police officers to accost you on the street if you have done nothing wrong. Therefore, if someone flashes a badge and begins to ask you questions, especially if s/he is in plain clothes, be very wary. If you're in a populated area and the ID looks legitimate (check it!), and the questions are not personal in nature, you may choose to answer the questions.

2) Under no circumstances should you get into a vehicle or go to any secondary location with a suspect officer without confirming his identity via 911 on your cell phone. Ask for a uniform patrol car to transport you rather than getting into an unmarked vehicle.

3) If you do end up in a vehicle and your abductors' words or actions tell you that they are not real police officers, crash the car.

4) If a car that does not appear to be a uniform patrol car (e.g. single roof or dash light as opposed to a large array of flashing lights and markings) asks you to pull over in an isolated area, do not stop. Signal the car to follow you and drive until you reach a populated or secure location (NOT your home). Keep your car in drive, foot on the brake, windows closed, door locked as the suspect officer approaches. Ask him to request a uniform patrol car be sent for your safety. Have your cell phone out and visible, ready to call 911. If he becomes violent or does anything that rings your alarm bells, hit 911 and the gas.

5) If you receive a phone call from someone claiming to be a police officer requesting information, ask for the phone number of his precinct and call back. You can check the authenticity of the phone number via the Internet.

Avoiding Purse Snatchers and Muggers

1) It's a good idea to carry valuables (license, keys, etc.) in a concealed location, not in your purse or wallet. That way, if someone threatens you and demands your possessions and you can't immediately escape, you can quickly give him your wallet or purse without losing too much. Few robbers will want to hang around to determine exactly what they've got after robbing you. Most will let you go once you've given up your purse or wallet, unless they have something more sinister in mind.

2) If your purse gets snatched, let it go, *don't get into a tug-of-war*. It's not worth risking severe injury or death to protect what's inside it.

3) **When out walking, *don't stop for anyone*.** Politely but firmly refuse requests for money, the time, directions, etc. as you keep moving and staying aware of your surroundings. You never know when someone may be trying to assess you or set you up for a robbery or worse. He may also be trying to distract you so that his accomplices can jump you from another direction.

4) If he tries to physically stop you, evade him and RUN. If this is not possible or if you're cornered, you must attack the attackers immediately and vehemently until you can escape.

Home Self-Defense

A great percentage of violent crimes occur in the home. Many of these are perpetrated by co-inhabitants of the victims, or by people the victims invite inside. Avoiding abusive relationships is outside the scope of this book (see "The Gift of Fear" by DeBecker), but as a rule, don't invite anyone into your home whom you do not know and trust very well. To keep uninvited guests out of your home, here are some tips:

1) Get a dog suitable for guard duty (research which breeds work best). Few burglars or home invaders are willing to tangle with a dog.

2) To cover the outside of your home, install motion sensor lights and keep all windows and doors clear of bushes and trees. Get a timer for your lights and TV when away.

3) To help protect the inside, make sure all doors and windows (including the garage door) are secure and kept locked. Install a good alarm system with multiple redundancies (motion and glass break sensors, wireless window switches and barrier bars). Local companies with a long history in an area and many positive recommendations are often more reliable than large national companies. Do your research. Make sure you can clearly see anyone on your doorstep from inside the house via a peep sight, camera system, etc. Don't open your door to anyone you don't know or aren't expecting. Criminals often use ruses to gain entry, posing as repairmen, mail carriers, etc. *They may even feign an emergency or use women and children to get you to open the door.* Don't do it—just call 911 to summon help.

4) **If home invaders have made it past your motion lights, locks, alarm, dog and any other measures, you have a serious problem to deal with.** Make your bedroom your hardened "fallback room" with a secure door and lock. Door jam bars are best. Inside, keep a charged cell phone so that you can bypass cut phone lines to call 911, and a pump-action 20- or 12-gauge shotgun in case the intruders get through the door. No sane person will keep coming after hearing the shotgun being racked. If they do breach the bedroom door, don't hesitate to empty the shotgun into them. In case you don't have time to get everyone into the bedroom during a lighting-fast home invasion, it is best to carry a large-capacity handgun (with which you are licensed and trained) on your person while you are at home. You may usually legally do this on your private property even if you don't have a carry permit (check local laws to be sure).

5) Having other people in the home to protect, especially children, can complicate things tremendously. Immediate escape is the best defense. Practice a home evacuation plan that involves your entire family. If your perimeter is breached, everybody should try to get out through the nearest window or door and get a neighbor's attention.

6) Don't leave valuables within sight of the windows. Keep curtains closed when possible.

21

7) Never enter your home if you have reason to suspect there's been a break-in (e.g. damaged door or window frame, key won't fit in lock). Leave the area and call 911 to have the police check it out.

8) If you're out walking or driving, and your awareness picks up a person or vehicle you suspect is following you, confirm the tail by circling a block to see if the person or vehicle continues to follow you. Anyone NOT following you would have no reason to circle a block and continue in the original direction. Don't go home, lest you be attacked in your driveway or doorway. Drive or walk towards the nearest police or fire station or densely populated area while calling 911 on your cell phone.

Staying Safe While Jogging

Jogging is always safer if you can do it during daylight, with friends, along a popular route free from nearby shadows or bushes or other good concealment points. Pepper spray is frequently recommended for joggers. Just be aware that it is far from 100% effective (more like 50% in John Perkins' experience, and that's when used properly), especially against enraged, drugged or determined attackers. It can, however, be useful when combined with good tactics. Spray while moving to escape, or spray, hit and escape. Don't just stand there and expect the bad guy to drop when sprayed. Prior self-exposure to pepper spray will make you better able to continue to function and escape in case the spray blows back at you or is transferred to you from your attacker's skin. Be sure to do this outside, with decontaminant, soap and water and medical assistance immediately available. Also:

1) **Never wear headphones in public.** They cut off much of your awareness.
2) Try to give at least a 10-foot berth to parked cars, buildings, corners and other possible ambush points. You will need this space and time to react in case someone tries to jump you.
3) Avoid a predictable jogging schedule. Don't allow a predator to plan your ambush.
4) A personal alarm that you can set off with one hand may help attract attention if you're attacked.
5) If you feel you're being followed, see above. Keep moving and call 911.

Key Points:
--Trust your instincts; don't get into a bad situation in the first place
--You're on your own; only you can save you
--Cops are not going to be there to help you

II CHALLENGE NO ONE

Looking to fight is beyond stupidity for 2 reasons: 1- Even if you win you can be severely injured (and die later) and 2- You never know whom you're dealing with.

Fight Story: You Never Know Whom You're Dealing With

Author Matt Kovsky was attending his High School reunion many years ago when a short man pushed past him while entering a door. Kovsky was knocked into the wall and said, "Hey watch it!" The short man screamed back "F*#k you asshole!" Kovsky was stepping forward, sensing he could crush the punk, when a third person intervened and de-escalated the situation. (He knew the punk's brother). Afterwards, Kovsky said to the third person "Why did you stop me? I could've kicked his ass!" He replied, "Because everybody in the neighborhood knows that punk just got himself a new gun and he's been itching to try it out."

Forget about honor, machismo or needing to "represent." Adopting a "Challenge No One" philosophy has three advantages that need to be stressed repeatedly:
1) **You avoid petty squabbles and later entanglement with the legal system.**
2) **It restricts fights to those you *absolutely must* undertake to save your life.**
3) **It relieves you of the moral indecision and guilt when you have no other choice but to do what must be done. This mindset alone triples your fighting power.**

Fight Story: You Never Know What Can Happen

Years ago, John Perkins had a female student who was a competitive kick boxer. One day while she was walking in the city a homeless person attacked her. She unleashed a barrage of kicks and punches and knocked him to the ground. Unfortunately, instead of leaving *immediately*, she leaned over him to see if he was ok. The homeless man suddenly rolled over and stabbed her in the face with a punch knife. She survived, but it took extensive reconstructive surgery and many years for her to recover. The lesson here is to do what you have to and run. Police statistics show that weapons don't usually enter the situation until the fight is already underway.

Similarly, your idiot "friends" can suck you into a fight not of your choosing in bars, at sporting events, etc. where the end result is incarceration, injury, death and a permanently ruined life. If this sounds familiar, you'd better get NEW friends. Fast.

Less-Than-Lethal vs. Lethal Tactics Training: The Baseball Bat Analogy

You only fight to save your life or a loved one's. That's it. Not to salvage a wounded ego, prove your machismo, or defend your or someone else's honor or reputation. When you eliminate all the remarkably stupid-ass fights people become involved in over the course of a lifetime (especially during your utterly moronic and alcohol-addled twenties and teen years), what you are left with are true life and death situations that are the moral equivalent of War. As we say, this eliminates that moral gray area where you may be thinking "Well...I'll hit/grapple him until he says 'uncle' or until he knows I'm the better man." Forget that crap. You need to prepare your mind to Kill the Enemy and take him off the planet with whatever means necessary to save your life. *This is because you were forced into it with no opportunity to run away.*

This internal dialogue is important because it dictates what tactics you will use to defend yourself: **less-than-lethal** (i.e. controlling maneuvers: locks, holds, grapples; non-penetrating strikes: punches to the nose, stomach, chest) or **lethal** (strikes to the neck, throat, gouges to the eyes, etc.)

But isn't it safer for everyone concerned to use less-than-lethal tactics? No, it is not. Consider the Baseball Bat Analogy:

If you always practice hitting a child's plastic baseball with a plastic wiffle-ball bat, what happens if one day you have to play at Yankee Stadium with a real Louisville Slugger facing Major League fastballs? You'll strike out every time. What if someday a Meth-crazed psychopath attacks you in your own home at night, with your wife and kids present? Are you going to punch him, mount him and place him in an arm lock? Really? Stop watching so much TV. *You're going to have to rip out his windpipe and drive your fingers so deeply into his eye sockets that they meet inside his brain.* Literally. So where does the Baseball Bat Analogy

26

come in? If you train with a real bat against major league pitching you can always <u>bunt</u> if you need to instead of swinging for the fences. But if all you know is swinging at plastic baseballs with plastic wiffle-ball bats (or sparring with wrist locks and sportive hitting), you're a dead man. Literally.

With lethal tactics you can always back off as necessary. The reverse is never true. You can't ramp up less-than-lethal tactics and expect them to save your life when it really counts.

This, by the way, also has applications to law enforcement: a cop who doesn't know how to fight to save his life and must "play" with his academy-trained controlling tactics will be more likely to resort to his sidearm when his controlling tactics fail to control the perpetrator. This is where people get shot unnecessarily. So training lethal tactics can actually wind up being safer for both cop *and* criminal.

Key Points:
- **Self defense is about life and death, not your pride or ego**
- **In a real fight you must win, 2nd place results in death**
- **Even when you win a real fight you can still be injured**
- **If you have to fight it is all or nothing**
- **You're either in the fight or you're not, there is no middle ground**

III THE PERSONAL COMFORT ZONE/SPHERE OF INFLUENCE

Establish a personal comfort zone that no stranger is allowed to enter. In prison they say: "Give me 5 feet MUTHAF#CKA!" to avoid getting stabbed. This is not paranoia, just good practical sense. **You need a trigger that allows you to stay relaxed most of the time.** At a minimum, the zone is about as far as you can extend your arm. This is also known as your Sphere of Influence. Your Sphere of Influence refers to the balanced, body-unitized limit you can comfortably reach with your hand and foot weapons. You never fight outside of your Sphere. This means you never over-extend or unbalance yourself. If you have to step, step and take your whole balanced, body-unitized Sphere with you. Maintaining this Sphere or Personal Comfort Zone may require that you walk around people so they don't get too close. Refusing to give space needlessly is a senseless provocation and another liability of so-called assertiveness training. Don't create or let yourself be pulled into senseless confrontations. You never know whom you are dealing with. Maintaining your personal comfort zone is difficult in a crowded subway or elevator, but in these situations your awareness is already heightened. Also, potential attackers are discouraged from attacking in such crowded conditions: there are witnesses, and the attacker's escape route is usually obstructed.

Awareness Concepts and your Sphere of Influence

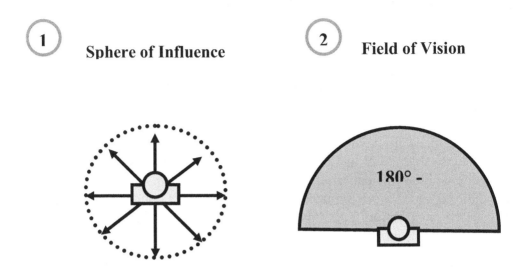

Figure 1 is the Sphere of Influence. In Figure 2 you can see that we have drawn an arc which covers between 180° to 205° degrees and represents your field of vision including your peripheral vision. Both of these rely on what is called your sub-cortical vision or as we like to say "Spatial Awareness." Spatial Awareness is nothing more than the ability to judge spatial relationships in time and space relative to your location. Your field of vision is a part of your spatial awareness and is what allows you to react to what you see in relation to your body before a person is able to enter your Sphere of Influence.

Below in Figure 3 you can see that the diagrams have been combined; this is because they both work together. Spatial Awareness or sub-cortical vision extends as far as your field of vision permits. This is your first line of defense before the enemy enters your Sphere of Influence. Now stay with us here. Focusing outward creates an invisible zone around you like radar which allows you to become more aware of what is going on *before* a person has a chance to get close enough to affect you. **This "radar" is useless, however, *unless you act on it!***

Anyone that enters this zone is fair game and just by merely changing your body position or stepping off line or moving you can thwart their initial attack angle. Because you have already observed them, in order for them to get their stuff off they will either have to suddenly move toward you or use some form of verbal subterfuge to put you at ease and get the drop on you. Now you understand why criminals use the "Interview" technique (explained later, with drills). It allows them to get close to people without setting off the warning signs a rapid approach would cause. Point being, if your mind is focused outward, it's just not that easy for someone to walk up and attack you.

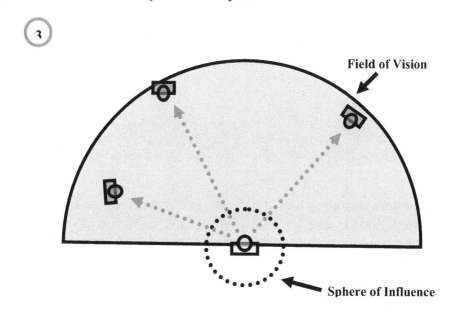

Field of Vision

Sphere of Influence

Field of Vision Looking Outward

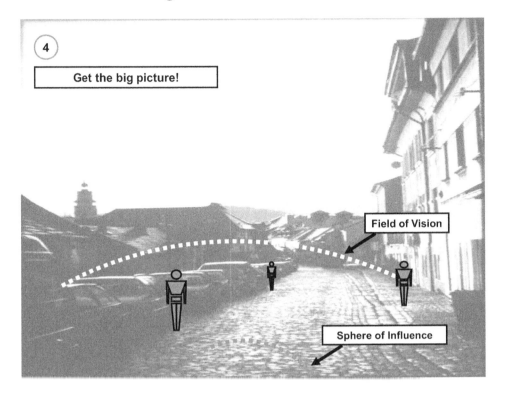

Figure 4 above shows how this works in a real setting such as on a street. The top dotted line represents your field of vision looking outward "getting the big picture" while the bottom dotted line represents your Sphere of Influence (the range limit of your weapons). The figures represent potential attackers. Remember that distance equals time and the sooner you can observe their actions, and the greater the distance they have to cover, the more time it allows you to react to or pre-empt their actions. Though this is an oversimplification you get the idea.

Think of it like this: in bar room brawls, if a person can avoid the initial onrush of their attacker (especially a sucker punch) the person launching the attack almost always over commits, making your defense easier. However, if they connect, they almost always win. By using awareness to scope things out and observe what people are doing, you buy time for yourself to react. Even a few seconds is like an eternity in a real fight. This concept works the same way as maintaining a safe following distance in your car as opposed to tailgating. The closer you are and the faster the speed, the less time you have to react. It's simply action/reaction.

Sphere of Influence, Continued

Sphere of Influence

Transition your Root
Forward or Back

In the diagram above we see that our "Sphere of Influence" extends to the maximum range of where we can strike with effectiveness (Fig 5). Because our limbs are just long enough to protect our bodies, regardless of body type we want to learn to fight within our own sphere. Fig 6 above shows the relationship between balance and your sphere of influence while controlling your equilibrium as you transition your root between your front and back leg without stepping. Notice that as you "root" (transfer your weight) forward and back, as long as you don't blow your balance by overextending, you're able to move your sphere accordingly while maintaining control over your weapons.

Step to a new Root

If your attacker is just beyond the range where you can effectively strike him (even if you root on the forward leg) do not overextend and lose balance. Step forward to a new root point as shown above in Fig 7 and move your sphere of influence, maintaining control over your limbs. **Also, NEVER visualize blasting all the way through the enemy as this almost guarantees you will lose balance (especially if you miss)!**

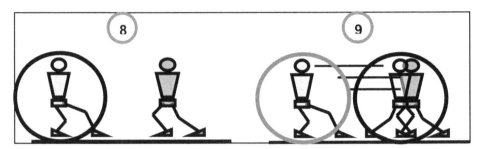

As shown above in Fig's 8 & 9, by moving your center of gravity with you as you step to a new root point it enables you to always strike with maximum power and cutting force because you are able to penetrate their center. Notice the distance you cover as you move forward from your root point.   This is important because it requires that the person you are stepping towards move much faster to get out of the way and move their sphere as well. If he tries to run he can't move backwards fast enough because you stepped in first and cut off all possible escape angles, making you unavoidable.

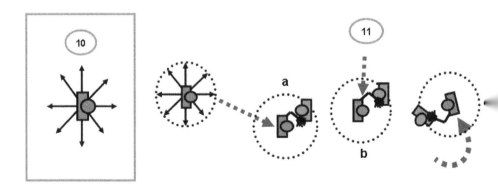

Finally, no matter which direction you turn or step, your sphere of influence goes with you and remains the same along with your center of gravity. So no matter which way you line your weapons up you are able to strike in every direction with power. This is a function of balance. Fig 10 provides a basic understanding of the different directions to which you can step. Fig 11 shows the relationship between your Sphere of Influence and how you can control your center of gravity as you step. For example, you can step forward (Fig 11a) slightly off line into an opponent, switch feet as in Fig 11b (perhaps stepping off line as you kick) or box step (see the Box Step chapter) around him and strike him from the side or even better, from the rear (as shown in Fig 11c). Notice as you step your sphere travels with you. The key is you want to trap him within your sphere so that it's not so much that you hit him, as it is his body just gets in the way of your weapons. This is important because even if you miss (for whatever reason) because you are still fighting within your sphere and on balance, you can quickly recover and strike from another angle as necessary. **In a nutshell: Never reach, lean, or over-commit your balance to a strike.**

The "Mobile PCZ" Drill

Take your Personal Comfort Zone with you.

Give adequate space to people on the street. Don't have an obnoxious attitude of "I'M WALKIN' HERE--SO GET OUTTA MY WAY"...or trouble will certainly find you. As you pass a person closely, raise your closest arm to scratch your head, fix your hair, etc. This is a partial "Fright Reaction" position (explained later) that can help prevent or defend against a sudden side or rear attack from locking down on your throat.

Your PCZ goes with you wherever you are. As part of your Hostile Awareness Visualization training (coming up), practice walking on crowded sidewalks. Without acting like they have tuberculosis, give other pedestrians a wide enough berth as you pass them to take them to the outer limit of your own PCZ. Just as you pass them, raise your inside arm as if scratching your head. Obviously you can't do this for everyone but it develops good habits. As we will discuss soon, from this position you can defend against sudden throat and head attacks from the side and rear.

Key Points:

— First Line of Defense: Awareness

— Second Line of Defense: Field of Vision

— Third Line of Defense: Personal Comfort Zone

— Establish and maintain your Personal Comfort Zone. Allow no one to enter it uninvited. Move to keep people from entering it. Despite your obvious avoidance, *if they still seek to enter it even though you are giving them space,* Attack the Attacker (next chapter). They have crossed the Rubicon and are now within your Sphere of Influence

— You must control your sphere of influence at all times. *The sphere of influence concept insures that you never over-extend your weapons or over-commit your balance.*

— Maintain balance as you move

— Get the "big picture" and focus outward not inward

— Distance equals time and the sooner you can observe the enemy's actions, and the greater the distance they have to cover, the more time it allows you to react to or pre-empt their actions

— Our limbs are just long enough to protect our bodies. Regardless of body type, we must learn to fight within our own sphere of influence

— No matter which direction you turn or step, your sphere of influence remains the same along with your center of gravity

IV ATTACK THE ATTACKER

"Attacking the attacker" is a phrase coined by Bradley Steiner, President of the International Combat Martial Arts Federation. It refers to a philosophy of pre-emptive striking as your first line of self-defense. What triggers this is a stranger's (or hostile relation's) giving you a bad feeling and crossing the perimeter of your Personal Comfort Zone. This usually occurs during what's called the "Interview" phase of an assault. Remember that if the attacker's goal was just to stealthily assassinate you, there's no self-defense in the world that'll save you, short of a force field and an army of body guards, or a lot of luck. **We do extensive drilling of the Interview scenario later on.**

During the Interview, the criminal attempts to freeze you where you stand using eye contact and reassuring, shocking or distracting language. His goal is to bring down your guard and "check you out" for further criminal action (which may include a rear attack from an accomplice). Interview questions include but are not limited to:

1- "You got the time?"
2- "You got some change?"
3- "Do you know how to get to . . ?"

It may even involve invoking pity, using language like "I'm hungry, do you have any food?" It may involve *deliberate provocation* (usually used by punks seeking physical release--and *not necessarily* money, sex or a hostage) beginning with typical "what-you-gonna-do-about-it?" crap, etc.

Regardless, if your gut feeling (something you need to develop and trust) gives you the *slightest* distress, you:

1- say "Nothing," "No," or "I don't know" and *keep walking* or *back away*, but *keep your eyes on him*
2- scan around quickly for accomplices but snap your attention back to him
3- bring your hands up in a non-threatening "ready" stance (like the "Jack Benny" discussed elsewhere) that doesn't indicate you "know karate" and would welcome a fight.

Do not just turn your back on him and walk away or it could be the last thing you ever remember. By the way, if your gut instinct is overpowering, no one says you can't just flat out run away screaming. Your safety comes before a stranger's "feelings."

1. **"Sorry, I'm not interested." "Sorry, no time." "Sorry, I have no money,"** etc. *Keep walking* and quickly scan for accomplices. **(NOTE:** *You should maintain a GREATER distance than the compressed interval needed for the photo above. A PCZ should extend at least twice as far as you can extend your arm.***)**

READ, PRACTICE AND UNDERSTAND THE FOLLOWING:

Walking away is important both to maintain your PCZ and to **give the criminal every opportunity to avoid forcing you to explode in his face like a grenade.** If you give space and he keeps taking it, that's exactly what you're going to do by Attacking the Attacker. Retreating also removes that moral question of whether you should fight half-assed with restraint . . . or fight *like your life depends on it.* Such hesitation is the downfall of most victims of idiotic bar fights and other examples of immature macho stupidity. *You don't spar with the enemy.* You want to disable him instantly and run away. If a fight lasts longer than 4 seconds, *you're in trouble.* You need to be Aware and Avoid, Walk (or Run) Away or Fight for Your Life.

There is no in-between. You want to channel every ounce of adrenaline and effectively use it. Remember: A law-abiding person wouldn't keep pursuing you despite your withdrawal and verbal dismissal. If your life is in danger, your attack will involve throat and eye strikes that can be geared down as necessary. More on this concept coming up.

Key Points:

— **Never drop your guard**
— **Always give ground. Say "sorry, leave me alone, gotta go", etc.**
— **Scan around for accomplices**
— **Keep your hands up but *not* like you're ready to "fight."**
— **Never hesitate to strike when your PCZ is crossed**
— **Do not "spar"**
— **Go straight for the eyes and throat**
— **Strike first**
— **Strike to kill, scream, and *run away***
— **It is a waste of time to block since this may be the only opening you ever get (more on how to do this coming up)**
— **If the attacker reaches for you first, resist the temptation to stop his hand or grapple**

V VISUALIZATION

Developing Hostile Awareness

It would be nice if we all lived in a peace-loving utopia but unfortunately there are mutant scum among us who choose to prey upon the weak and unwary. You can choose to live in a dream world and hope that real violence is never visited upon you, but that is a crapshoot and, if the economy weakens, more people will choose crime as either a manifestation of their true natures or out of sheer economic desperation. No matter. Forewarned is forearmed. Some people will only seek self-protection training or prepare a home defense *after* they've been attacked or robbed. To quote another cliché, that's like closing the gate after the horse has left the barn. If your home is robbed, you will feel violated and a lot poorer. But you'll be okay. If it's a home invasion and you're home, or a street attack and you're crime-oblivious, you'll be injured, raped, crippled...or dead.

That being said, we're not suggesting you walk around on perpetual red alert. Simply take note of your surroundings when out in public and, as a casual mental exercise, calmly visualize dealing with attacks from people in your vicinity.

Try hostile awareness visualization on crowded sidewalks, busy streets, empty streets, subways, buses, in classrooms, workplaces, airliners, cars, everywhere. Could you run away? Which direction? Is there an escape route? How would they attack? From what angle? How would you strike? Are there environmental weapons you can pick up (rock, bottle, stick, pipe)? **Train yourself to look for them.** Do you have a sturdy metal pen easily accessible as a defensive stabbing weapon or to release chokes (by stabbing into the crook of the arm, hand or face if necessary)? Are your shoes sturdy enough for kicking? It is now possible to get steel toe shoes in virtually any style from sneaker to dress to casual so there's never an excuse not to have the equivalent of a sledgehammer on each foot, always at the ready.

The more you do this mental visualization drill in a calm, relaxed, playful manner, the more you are engaging in subconscious neural programming (something all elite athletes practice). Later, you can practice it under duress. Eventually it will become second nature and you will react appropriately if the spit hits the fan. Remember, we're not creating paranoia, mental dysfunction or unchecked hostility but the skill to recognize and react to danger *in your environment*. Failing to plan is planning to fail and crude anger without focus robs you of looseness and reactivity. You want to learn to *focus your adrenaline like a laser beam*, and that's what the "Focus Your Fear" meditation drill is all about. (There is a complete description of this drill in Attack Proof 2nd edition and on the Companion Part 1 DVD.)

Focus Your Fear

Go into an isolated safe room when no one is home (or as part of a self defense class exercise in a school). Close the windows, lock the door and turn off the lights. Stand relaxed with your arms at your sides and begin slow deep breathing into your *stomach* (chest breathing *raises* anxiety). As you breathe in, feel the power of the sun and the shared life force of all good livings things fill every cell of your body.

Feel your weight sinking into your feet and the rich, red energized blood pooling in your arms. Now...once you begin to feel powerful, calm and relaxed, begin to dredge up your worst memories of violence and humiliation, all the times you were wronged without the ability or opportunity to retaliate *(be VERY careful with this and consult your mental health practitioner first if you are currently undergoing therapy for PTSD or some other past trauma).*

Now, visualize the most vile psychopath imaginable holding you and the person you care about most in this world (or the most vulnerable, or a favorite pet, etc.), hostage. He's going to kill you. But FIRST he's going to torture your companion *right in front of you.*

Not if you can help it!

Take all that pain, fear and anger that's boiling a cauldron of adrenaline in your brain and guts and drive it deep into your feet. Keep breathing deeply without tension and visualize the bright white light of the Sun filling you with power and justice. Feel the power and adrenaline building.

Not if you can help it! **Pull the trigger and unleash the Dogs of War.** NOW IS THE TIME. Let the energy explode and rush up and out through your legs, hips, back, shoulders, arms, hands and mouth in the loudest, deepest, animal warrior shout you can muster, while your hands rip and tear at the air like a roaring mountain lion. Do this for a full five seconds.

Focus Your Fear: Feel the concentrated rage, terror and adrenaline come exploding up from the soles of your feet, through your body and out your hands and mouth with vicious strikes and an ear-splitting roar.

Now relax. Stand quietly with your arms at your sides and breathe slowly and evenly. Relax in the knowledge that you have a power source deep within you to save your life or a loved one's when necessary. It is always available. Soon you will also have the tools and the weaponry.

Focus Your Fear trains you to become familiar with, channel and release the potential paralysis that can occur when danger strikes.

You will learn to welcome the adrenaline of fear as your *friend*--a virtual nuclear furnace burning in your gut. You now know that you can explode and act when necessary and your family depends on it. With frequent practice, you will be able to tap this inner well of adrenaline energy and fear will begin to take on a completely different character—one of power and action instead of terror, paralysis and indecision.

Even after you've learned all the skills in this book, you should still practice Focus Your Fear at least once a week.

Do Not Go to Crime Scene #2

Part of developing a passive "Hostile Awareness" is understanding deep in your gut that you will never, ever go to Crime Scene #2. What is "Crime Scene #2"? Let's take a quiz:
If you're mugged or assaulted and the criminal wants to take you somewhere, do you:

       i. talk your way out of it
      ii. go along and wait for rescue
     iii. go along and escape later

The answer is none of the above. If the criminal wants more than or something other than money, you are now involved in a kidnapping, car-jacking, rape, abduction or hostage situation and your odds of survival are remote.

NEVER GO TO CRIME SCENE #2: Police statistics confirm that if you go with the attacker to another location, *the odds of being killed or being so severely tortured that you might wish you had been killed are extremely high.* However, they also show that if you either run immediately or fight for your life the odds are *reversed.*

Viewed from this perspective, your choices are simple:

1- If you're mugged for money, give it to him. Give him your whole wallet or purse and don't go rummaging around for bills. Be polite and respectful. Many "experts" say you can throw your wallet in one direction and run in the other, but some psycho may get pissed off and casually blow you away...and *then* retrieve your wallet!

2- If they want to take you someplace, you're going to have to make your stand, right here, right now. How you do that is what we detail in this manual. Realize, however, that this is not a Hollywood movie and you probably won't get out of it uninjured. But if you run or fight back, you have a much better chance of surviving, with less injury, than if you're abducted.

3- If you are being forcibly restrained and are moved to a car or van, you will need to train how to fake being so debilitated by fear or medical emergency (e.g. paralysis, heart attack) that the criminal has to change his hold on you, giving you an opening to attack. Under the circumstances, the acting job probably won't be too far from the truth.

Key Points:
- — *Regularly* **practice the "Focus Your Fear" meditation drill to develop your nervous system, mind set, and ethical and moral resolve for the extreme violence required to save your life. The more you do it, the more natural (and less debilitating) it will feel.**
- — **Practice the Hostile Awareness drill regularly. Set in your mind before hand what you will do. Train yourself to look for environmental weapons and escape routes wherever you are.**
- — **The three linchpins of awareness are scan, avoid, and carry a cell phone**
- — **Be prepared to fight**

VI BASIC DROPPING EXPLANATION
FOR POWER DELIVERY

Dropping Concept: you can develop enormous power with no windup or chambering by using the Guided Chaos principle of Dropping. This allows ferocious hitting at close range or indeed at *any* distance along the path of a strike. It also does not require great muscular strength.

Dropping involves a sudden, total body spasm similar to a cough or sneeze where your diaphragm contracts convulsively.

To Drop: bend your knees about 1-4 inches as fast you can WITHOUT first rising. The beginning, middle and END of the knee bending should be so SUDDEN that your feet actually come off the ground for an instant. You could actually slip a piece of paper between your foot and the ground.

Why this generates power: your entire body's mass sinks rapidly to the ground but is interrupted by the abrupt end of the knee bending. Since your body is mostly water, the wavelike energy is reflected from the ground back up through your body and channeled out into whatever weapon you are striking with. This is also like snapping a whip. Make sure that you are not rising first as a preparation for dropping. Simply drop right where you are.

Dropping Energy will be used for every strike you will learn and especially the Fright Reaction.

BASIC FRIGHT REACTION

THE FRIGHT REACTION: Forget about fancy kung fu stances. At the slightest touch, drop your weight, spread your stance and raise your shoulders, arms and hands to protect your eyes, neck and throat.

Your body has an innate flinch reaction to surprise that is often suppressed by popular culture.

On the flip side, this natural reaction is often stylized and *neutered* by martial arts. Need proof? If someone shot off a firecracker right next to your ear or a bee flew into your eye what would you do? Go into a kung fu "kombat stance"? Put the bee in an arm-lock? Of course not. Your natural reaction would be to drop your body weight, raise your shoulders, arms and hands and lower your head in order to protect your most vital assets: your eyes, neck and brain. In GCC, instead of forcing your body under duress to adopt some ridiculous, stylized, martial arts pose, we go with what works *naturally* and reinforce it. This consists of rapidly bending the knees and lowering the body, widening the stance, raising the shoulders, sinking the head and raising the hands up behind the neck to protect the head and spine. The elbows should be pointing outwards like two spikes that an unwary attacker could become impaled upon (see photo above). It also prevents a rear choking attack from getting locked down since your hands are already in the way. The lowered body stance also provides the perfect platform for exploding into counter strikes.

We will work on the Fright Reaction within a series of scenario drills later on but for now, we wanted you to see how this most basic of movements relies on Dropping Energy.

Applying Dropping Energy to Striking

Now you will see how this same Dropping methodology applies to actual strikes.

Basic Drop-Striking Drill:

Stand relaxed with your arms extended in front of you. Now Drop almost exactly as you did with the Fright Reaction but with these differences:

1) Drop only an inch or two and don't widen your stance.
2) Keep your arms in the relaxed position extended in front of you without leaning. We are focusing here exclusively on the action of the knees.
3) The instant you stop the drop, relax and slowly straighten your knees to the start position. The Drop and the *stopping* of the drop are extremely sudden and take a microsecond; straightening the knees should take a full second or two. On each drop, try to get all the loose flesh on your body to shake as if jolted by an electric shock. This should be a byproduct of snapping your body with the abrupt cessation of the Drop. Repeat 10 times.
4) Now on each Drop, throw a short palm heel strike simultaneously with each hand (it should look like a short, sudden, snapping push). Try to time the strikes so that they occur not *on* the Drop (bending of the knees) but a microsecond after you *stop* the Drop. What you are trying to do is catch the plyometric "rebound" of your Dropping momentum as it reflects off the ground and back up your body. The sensation is very similar to a cough or sneeze except that instead of your breath exploding out of your mouth, your palm heel strikes explode from your arms, propelled by the bounce off your root. The strikes are short, snappy and extremely fast and take

51

some practice to perfect. How do you know if you're doing it right?

Dropping Compression Test

1) To test the suddenness and proper plyometric rebound effect of Dropping, stand relaxed with your arm extended out in front of you, parallel to the ground and slightly to the side. Place your palm lightly but *flat* on a solid brick wall.
2) Perform a Dropping palm heel strike as in the Basic Drop-Striking Drill above. Be sure that your palm *remains flat* on the wall *throughout the drill*. This is essential. Do not lean on the wall; remain relaxed the entire time except for the microsecond of the strike.
3) If you're doing this correctly, the suddenness of the Drop-strike reflected off the brick wall should feel like a jackhammer blasted through your shoulder and into your entire body, driving it away from the wall. It should be an effort to keep your palm flat and your hand and arm devoid of tension.
4) If you strike too early or too late, you won't "catch the wave" and will force tension into your body and lack the explosiveness that is intrinsic to proper Drop-striking.

Advantages of Drop Striking

1) It requires no windup
2) It can be delivered at close range
3) It has more power and speed than typical gross muscle striking
4) It keeps you relaxed, balanced and ready to "reload" and strike again
5) It can be used to "ricochet" into a barrage of further strikes (see Attack Proof 2nd edition for this advanced Guided Chaos concept).
6) When Dropping Energy is applied to *full-length* strikes, the amount of power generated as compared to typical muscle strikes is even more devastating. To get the most out of it, see "the Rocket Step" in Attack Proof 2nd edition.

Middle Line Backer Hitting Drill for Developing Dropping Energy

This drill takes the principles of the Basic Drop-Striking Drill and applies it to multiple rapid-fire striking. If you've played football you probably remember this one:

1) With your hands in front of you, pick your feet up and step in place as fast as you can.
2) Here's where we modify it: With each step, shoot out a palm heel strike with the alternate hand. In other words, as your right foot lands, hit with the left palm heel and vice versa.
3) Make your steps smaller and smaller and faster and faster until your feet are *barely* leaving the ground. You could call this the "supersonic shuffle." At the same time, try to keep your palm striking in sync with your steps.
4) Try this against a heavy bag. Try also coordinating palm strikes with the *same* side step (left hand step, left palm strike). At the highest speeds, your body will naturally fall into the best synchronization of hand and foot.

The point of this drill is to get you to put your entire body weight behind every strike. By stepping, you *force* this to happen. By taking smaller and faster steps, you increase your coordination and the ability to marshal all your power instantaneously and loosely without muscling up. **In essence, this is actually a high speed dropping drill** (a full explanation of Dropping with many more drills is in chapter 6 of Attack Proof as well as the Attackproof Companion Part 1 and Combat Conditioning DVDs).

Without Balance you have nothing: In order to develop the ability to drop on any strike the most important thing you must develop is *dynamic balance*. Without balance you can do nothing; you need to be able to "catch" and control your body as you strike, since the power emanates from your root through your center of gravity. As you drop you must land with your foot flat with your center of gravity rooted over the foot you drop on. Although this is beyond the scope of this GCC manual, the advancing martial artist should practice all the various balance and footwork exercises in Attack Proof 2nd edition and the Companion Part 2 DVD to maximize their balance development under chaotic combat conditions. This includes the Ninja, Vacuum and Crazy Walks.

Key Points:

— With the Middle-linebacker Hitting Drill, start off slowly, focusing on developing your timing and then gradually pick up speed

— When Dropping (such as with the Fright Reaction), resist the temptation to launch with your legs by jumping up in the air first

— Feel yourself rooting to the ground with each drop; knees are bent; do not hop forward or lean in any one direction. You drop straight down. This will ensure that as you strike you are able to do so with maximum contraction of the muscles and balance. It also prevents you from slipping on ice, blood or oil.

— Make sure as you recover before your next drop that you return to the original position. You should be totally *relaxed* immediately *after* and between each drop.

— Ensure that the hands are already in the proper position to make strikes work

— Drop and strike as fast as you can, making sure you remain balanced as you strike and relaxed in between strikes. The drills coming up reinforce this.

VII BASIC STRIKES AND TARGETS

> *"The most well made tools are worthless in the hands of those who are unskilled in their use..."*
> --Alexander the Great

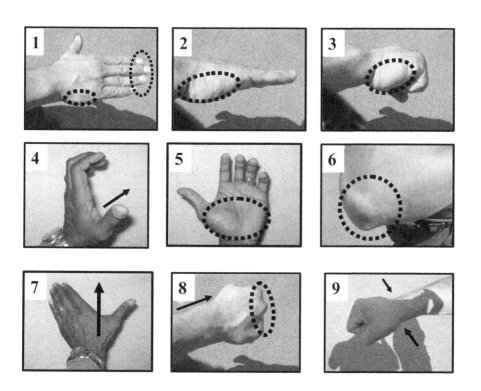

STRIKING TOOLS:

1. Spear hand and side of hand
[note in figure 1 the exaggeration of the "thumb." This is critical when striking with the side of the hand. Whcn using the spear hand the thumb can be against the hand.]
2. Side of hand (knife hand/chop)
3. Hammer fist
4. Palm heel strike

5. Palm heel strike surface
6. Elbow strike
7. "Y" strike for the throat
8. Regular fist strike is generally used on the body and soft parts of the head and neck. Though made popular in sport fighting it is generally the least effective bare handed fighting tool for real combat.

Note: the wrist is weak and breaks easily in a regular punch and takes years to develop. This is why boxers wrap their wrists before fights. More on this coming up.

Kicking

Use only the toe (preferably with steel-toed footwear) or heel for kicking. Using the sole or blade of the foot is much less powerful and increases the risk of ankle and metatarsal injuries during training and especially when fighting to save your life. Keep the foot at a 90° angle to the leg to provide mechanical advantage and structural integrity.

As we mention throughout this manual, steel and composite toe footwear is now available in virtually every style, from casual, to dress, to athletic. Wouldn't you prefer to kick with what essentially amounts to sledgehammers at the ends of your legs? Steel toe shoes are legal "weapons" that can go with you everywhere and requiring no permits. Go to steeltoeshoes.com and checkout their selection.

Primary Target Areas

Strikes to these areas (even with poor technique) can cause severe injury or even death. It should be noted that contrary to popular belief, strikes to the abdomen may require repeated striking since this area generally has more give than the head and neck. Finally, do not ever assume that one shot will be sufficient to take someone out (especially body shots). It may be necessary (especially if they are under the influence of drugs) to strike these areas repeatedly.

1. Eyes / bridge of nose / temple area
2. Base of skull / neck
3. Throat / neck
4. Ribs / sternum / abdomen
5. Groin
6. Sciatic nerve
7. Front/ back / side of knees
8. Shin / instep of foot
9. Achilles tendon

How to use the hands and where to focus the strikes [next page]

The Dots are the most vulnerable points on the body above the neck. The "Red" Zone [next page, boxed area to the left] is where you want to concentrate your striking. Regardless of size, if a person is struck in this area more than likely it will result in either death or some form of incapacitation of your attacker. The eyes and throat, the base of the skull, as well as the side of the neck are extremely vulnerable. For the lower body, focus on the groin, kidneys and abdomen as well as spine and tailbone.

While there are others (such as the knees) these are the primary areas that you want to target.

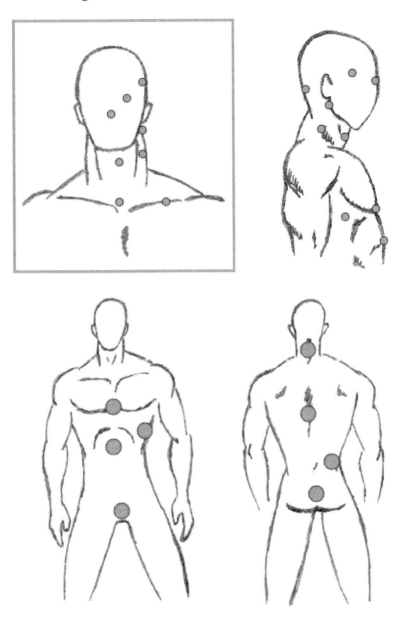

Many of the strikes detailed in this section can be lethal if practiced properly. They do not involve complicated movements. Most of them are culled from methods taught to United States soldiers during WWII to defeat the Japanese, who were all presumed to be skilled in judo, jujitsu, and karate.

ALWAYS PENETRATE THE CENTER OF THE TARGET

When hitting a target, never use a glancing strike. This will disrupt your balance, increase your chances of missing and lessen power substantially. Always hit *dead center*. This is true even if your strike is a hooking or roundhouse strike. Imagine a vertical line extending from the ceiling to the floor and dropping directly through the center mass of the body part you're hitting. *Hit through this line on every strike.* If every time you hit a heavy bag it spins, you know you have a lot of work to do. The bag should dent or fold with absolutely no rotation if you're hitting correctly.

Striking Center Mass on the Heavy Bag "the Correct Way"

When striking the heavy bag one thing you want to do is learn how to penetrate the center of the bag from every possible angle.

In Fig-1a, you can see the fist striking the bag in relation to the center mass of the bag represented by the "black dot". Where the lines bisect corresponds to the bags center.

In Fig-1b, here this is presented a little better. Notice the alignment of the fist to the bag and the body in relation to the fist. When you strike you not only want to strike through the center of objects but also you want to align "your" center of gravity as best you can in relation to where you are striking. This will ensue that you are able to strike with the maximum mechanical advantage when penetrating the bag.

Fig - 1

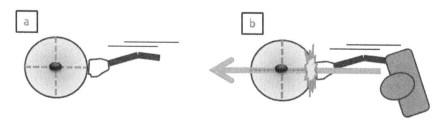

59

In Fig's-2a &b you can see that if you strike the bag to one side or the other because you are not striking through the center mass of the bag the rotational force causes the bag to spin.

This is a common error when people are first learning to strike the heavy bag and is the source of many a sprained wrist.

Fig - 2

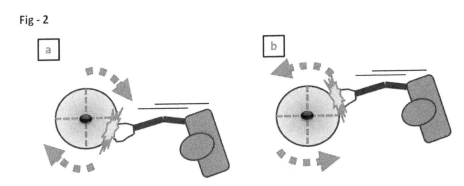

When practicing your striking start off <u>slow and easy "feeling" the center of the bag</u> as you strike. As you become more proficient you want to begin to "Drop Strike" on the bag, focus on "denting" the bag when dropping. While the below example [Fig-3b] greatly exaggerates this, you only need to penetrate the heavy bag an in or two to achieve the desired effect.

Fig - 3

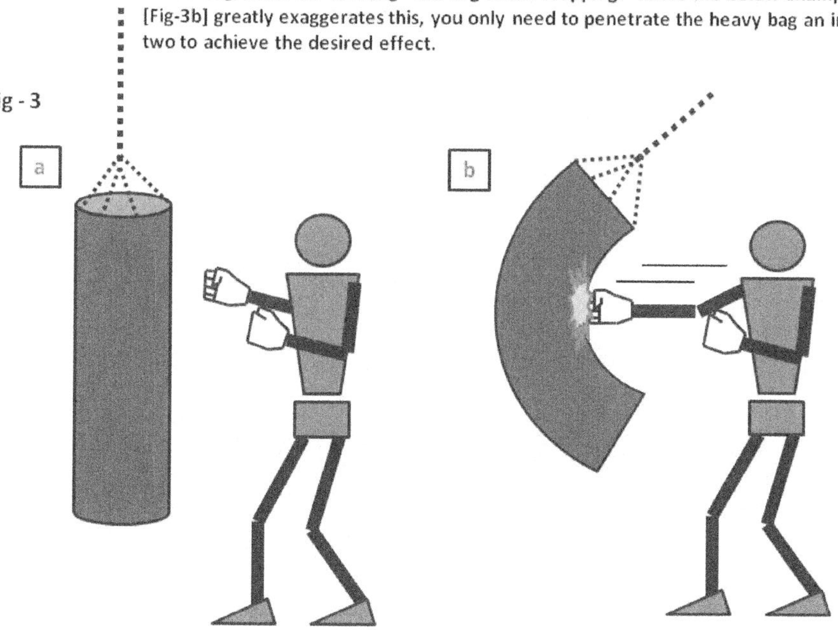

a

b

Final note, when striking you want to avoid pushing the bag [Fig-4]. While this looks cool in the gym and makes a lot of noise all you are doing is performing a lot of needless motion, and achieving more of a pushing effect that cutting or penetrating effect.

Fig - 4

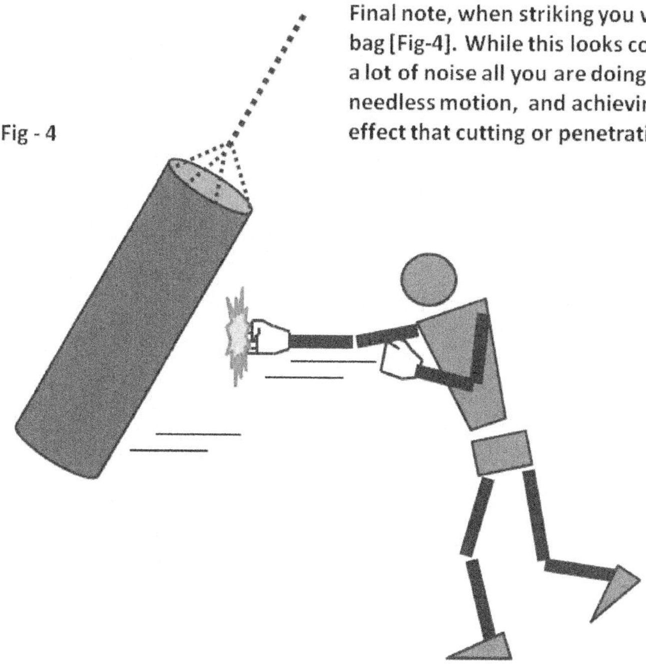

61

--Penetrate the bag only to the depth of a few inches.
--Do not over commit.
--Penetrate and cut the bag. Do not do pushing strikes.

Chin Jab (Palm Heel Strike)/Face Rip

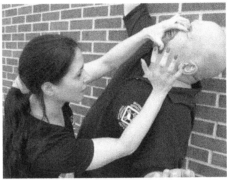

By smashing the heel of the palm straight up under the chin as if throwing a shot put or (banana cream pie!), you can disable or even kill a person because you are throwing the head back and disrupting vertebrae while rupturing the spinal cord.

But the mayhem doesn't stop there: the palm heel should have a **crushing/snatching** action so that in the midst of jarring the chin the fingers extend and gouge/rip deep into the eye sockets (smash in/snatch out). Practiced correctly, *this should in no way slow down the speed of the strike*. This is extreme but remember: you're fighting to save your life when you think you or a loved one could be killed. *There is never any other reason to fight.* Considering that *anything* can happen during a fight, *looking to fight* is actually beyond stupid.

> **Common error:** getting too close to the target so that you wind up crimping your shots, using only your triceps for power. On all strikes, learn to hit with your entire body, using a straight line of power from your feet through your hips, back, shoulders and arms.

Don't get too close! It crimps power. Hit with maximum extension without hyper-extending the elbows. Drive from your legs.

KEY POINTS:

--Try to time your strike so it coincides with the recoil (wave reflection of the drop off the floor as you halt the drop). This is akin to the snap of a whip.
--Do not crowd the target.
--Hit straight through the target center. No glancing strikes. Rip the leather from the bag.
--Ricochet off target; DO NOT PUSH.

EXTREMELY IMPORTANT: *"CONTAIN THE OVER-TRAVEL."* Do NOT rely or lean on your opponent's structure to support you! Never over-commit or over hit. You *visualize* penetrating several inches into the enemy's body mass target, but *never all the way through and out the other side!* This is a fatal flaw of many styles: if the opponent moves or you miss, slip or if he's simply tougher than you thought, your over-commitment to the strike will have you on your ass in a flash. Develop and deliver your strikes from your *own* root, using your *own* balance. This is why in the more advanced Guided Chaos, we spend so much time working on balance drills (Attack Proof 2nd edition, Companion Part 2 DVD, Combat Conditioning DVD). For the purposes of GCC though, it is enough to know that you *never* over-extend your strike; *you bring your Sphere of Influence with you* (previous chapter) and "contain your over-travel" using Dropping Energy.

Chops

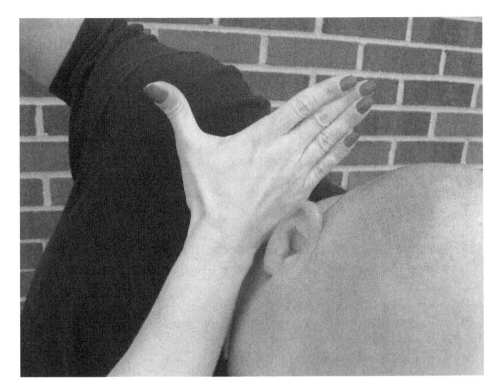

Chops delivered properly are devastating. With your hand held flat like an ax blade and your thumb extended 90 degrees (*not* held against the fingers like in karate) strike the back of the neck at the base of the skull, windpipe, eyes or the side of the neck. *The extended thumb position allows your arm muscles to relax and hit with more speed and power than traditional positions.* At the instant of impact you can stretch/shoot your fingers out which will instantaneously rigidify the weapon. The hand immediately relaxes a microsecond after impact but retains the initial shape. Use the fleshy part of the edge of the hand below the pinkie for hitting. You can also hit with the bony edge of the wrist or forearm. Use the entire loose weight of your body in the chop so it lands like a guillotine. Chops are amazingly versatile and can be delivered at virtually any angle to any part of the body. They also fold easily into elbow strike follow-up combinations, and vice versa. *For example: a right horizontal chop to the windpipe cutting right is easily followed by a right horizontal elbow smashing left (inwards) to the jaw hinge or temple.*

Practice combining chops and elbows within the same motion with the same arm. The same holds true for palm strikes and elbows strikes. In this case, for example, a right palm heel moving straight in or crashing from right to left just collapses into a right elbow also moving from right to left.

Spear Hand Strikes

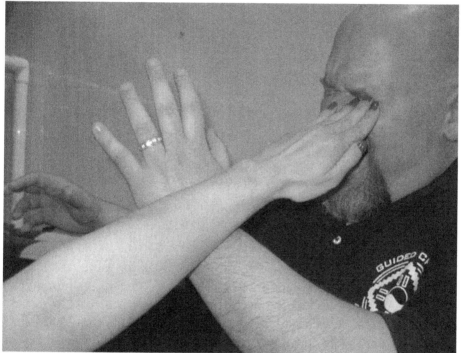

With your fingers together and almost straight, spear into the eyes and throat. This works on the biggest and strongest aggressors because there's no way any human being's eyelids can withstand a spear hand or eye gouge attack, even if they had steroids for breakfast. Some styles claim otherwise (they say you can "train and strengthen" the eyelids!) but the eyelids actually have all the resilience of a strip of uncooked bacon, no matter how much you train them.

Yoking, "V" or "Y" Strike

Despite the different names, they're all the same: with the hand in the chopping position, thrust the V shaped groove between the thumb and index finger into the windpipe of the attacker. Hit and pull back like a jackhammer. Y strikes are easy follow-ups, by the way, to palm strikes to the chest: just slide up and yoke the attacker.

Rips and Tears

At the very least, rips and tears can create openings for more devastating strikes when your other weaponry is unavailable (due to positioning or grappling). At best, they can be used to literally tear someone to pieces. You gouge, shred, squeeze, twist, rip and scratch soft body tissue using nothing but your hands and fingers. This is one of those few instances in Guided Chaos where we absolutely recommend strength training. Ideal regimens are Slambag, weighted wrist rolls (forward and reverse), sand bucket and mop handle training (all described in detail in Attack Proof and the Companion DVDs). Targets are the neck, groin, fingers, lips, hair, ears, eyes, throat, as well as loose flesh around the mouth, underarms (corner of the pectoral muscle), waist, etc. Note that this works better on some body types than others. It's actually easier to grab flesh on some ectomorphs than on some endomorphs. The muscles on some mesomorphs provide terrific handles for ripping and shredding.

Practice combined palm heel/rips on a BOB or focus pad so that you are actually trying to "snatch" or rip the leather from the face of the pad on retraction. DO NOT PUSH. Think of crushing a cockroach on a red-hot frying pan, then snatching it off fast enough so that you aren't burned, all in one fluid, pounding, shredding motion with dropping energy. Guided Chaos Slambag training is a complete methodology that is ideal for this but is beyond the scope of this manual. See attackproof.com for more info.

Claw

Rip at the eyes, face or any loose, vulnerable areas of flesh on the body as if you were a bear or tiger. Your fingers should not be pressed together. A claw strike to the face also doubles as a palm heel strike from its momentum.

Bites

Even if your arms are completely immobilized you can often do horrific damage by tearing into *any* available flesh with your teeth like a rabid dog. If it's life or death, all squeamishness will quickly go away. Worry about diseases later. You can't take antibiotics if you're dead. Try practicing gently against a headlock where your head is locked against the attacker's trunk.

Head Butts

Straight on head butt [Photo left]. You can also hit up under the chin. Roundhouse head butt delivered to jaw hinge [photo right].

Head butts are stunningly effective close range weapons, useful when your other weapons are unavailable or as an adjunct. The *only* part of the head to use is the front middle of the forehead right at the hairline (or where it *used* to be before you got "old"...or became a Marine!). If you use other parts of the head, you could get more messed up than your assailant.

Obviously don't hit the same point on *his* head (unless you're a moose…and not even then). Targets are the jaw, temple, nose, eye socket, etc. The head butt can be delivered upwards into a taller person or like a roundhouse punch into the side of his head.

Be VERY CAREFUL and gentle practicing head butts on a BOB or heavy bag because the head is extremely susceptible to brain damage.

Elbow Strikes

Elbows are one of the most deceptive and versatile weapons because they can be applied to almost any part of the body at virtually any angle with devastating effect. Their only limitation is range and you must be careful not to over extend yourself employing them because it can leave you very open. Practice on a BOB is extremely rewarding as you can do not only upward, downward and sideways strikes but also horizontal and vertical spearing strikes (use a long sleeved shirt or elbow pads when performing full power strikes on a BOB to prevent bleeding). Practice combining with chops and palm strikes.

Up elbow strike

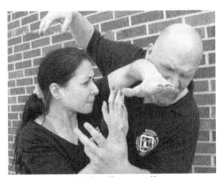
Side elbow strike

Spearing vertical elbow strike

Reverse elbow strike

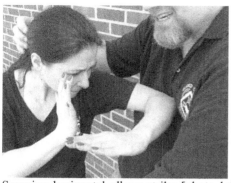 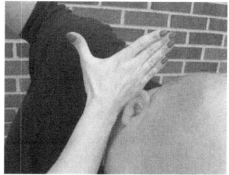

Spearing horizontal elbow strike [photo left]. Chops can flow right out of elbows and vice versa

Closed-fist Strikes

You could *palm* a brick wall full force…or *chop* a brick wall full force…

So why can't you *punch* a brick wall full force? Because you'd break your hand! Punching skulls is no different.

Surprise. We left regular punches for last because they're actually one of the *least* effective strikes because of many factors:

1- Few people beyond professional boxers *really* know how to make a proper, tight fist—and even they tape their wrists so they won't get broken!

2- The fist has many small bones cushioned by tendons and connective tissues acting as shock absorbers, thus reducing impact. In addition, the wrist can flex, twist and break, as in 1 above. Compare with chops and palm heels which are essentially bones sitting on top of bones, giving direct lines of power.

3- You can chop or palm heel a brick wall full power without too much damage (though we definitely do not advise it). Could you do that with a punch? Of course not. You'd break every knuckle in your hand as well as fracture your wrist. It's not much different hitting someone in the skull. Save regular punches for the liver, kidneys and other soft targets.

If you *do* punch, keep the hand loose until the moment of impact; then tighten the hand dramatically for a split second—and relax again. The action is similar to snapping a whip (like most strikes in Guided Chaos). This creates a "splashing" or rupturing effect on the body that is more effective than a pushing or straight, muscle-driven punch.

The type of punch we *do* recommend for everything is not a knuckle punch—it's a hammer fist. With a hammer fist, the striking surface is virtually the same as a chop's—with all of the chop's advantages of power, solidity and versatility and none of the knuckle punch's shortcomings. In *Guided Chaos Combat Boxing,* regular punches are used to destroy limbs, not skulls.

The hammerfist can be used on virtually any target with none of the knuckle punch's drawbacks.

Groin Strikes: How Effective Are They?

Despite what most people think (conditioned by TV and movies), groin strikes may not be effective against a truly enraged, adrenalized or drug-fueled maniac. Using groin strikes can be a particularly bad strategy for women (depending on the emotional and physical state of the attacker) because it may just piss him off. It *is* very effective on average, sober pests. The reason we bring this up is because if your life is in danger there are only two truly effective "pressure points" (despite what some martial arts "masters" claim) that have *real stopping power:* **the eyes and throat.** Nevertheless, it is *still* important to train groin strikes with the hand. Most trainees avoid it but it has to be included because "the way you train is the way you fight." If you feel squeamish you can hit the thigh instead in practice but it *must* be done to ingrain the weapon into your repertoire. This training includes both offense and defense (the defensive aspect of groin strikes is more properly addressed within Guided Chaos itself than in GC Combatives.)

When kicking to the groin, the strategy is to kick so hard that you blast into the groin and explode the whole pelvis--but without visualizing going *through* it. Going *through* the target is a common martial arts myth and methodology that encourages over commitment and upsets your balance--bad strategy for the crazy chaos of a real fight.

Knee Strikes

Targets: groin, tailbone, hips, thighs (inner and outer), side of knee, stomach, kidneys. To add power and speed, try to use a convulsive, diaphragmatic stomach contraction (similar to a cough) as opposed to isolated quadriceps muscles. Knee strikes should be low and not over-extended (like in kung fu movie knee shots to the head). Jumping up to knee the head will unbalance you and put you on your backside in a real fight.

Kicks and Stomps

In order not to telegraph kicks, they should be low, fast and unchambered. This means you should be able to launch the kick straight from the floor or wherever it originates without setting up or changing your stance. Dropping energy and the stomach contraction mentioned above helps, as does avoiding the high knee "chamber" (windup) associated with most karate styles. *Chambering wastes time and tells your attacker exactly what you're going to do,* a big handicap if you're going to seize a fleeting opening in their defense.

Stomps are important for 3 reasons:

1- It stabilizes you on oil, blood or ice.
2- It adds power to the next kick via the "ricocheting" principle (see Attack Proof).
3- It adds speed to the next kick because it effectively changes your root faster.
4- You can bust toes and insteps, which may stop a fight before it starts or create a huge opening as they convulse in pain.

NOTE: in all the Drop-step motions in the rest of this manual—such as The Prow, advanced CCUE or simply drop-step kicking—you can enhance the stomping speed and power by visualizing crushing a fast-moving cockroach with your lead foot before it gets away. This is a two-step movement similar to a compressed fencer's thrust).

DRILL: MEXICAN HAT DANCE against low heavy bag or kicking shield. [See Attack Proof p. 41 and the Companion DVD for a video demonstration]

You can call this drill anything you want but the image you want to come away with is rapid-fire machine gun kicks delivered low at close range while moving around your attacker. It winds up looking like a wild, foot-stomping dance as if you were trying to crush a scurrying hoard of cockroaches and kick them into roach hotels. Getting your toes smashed and shins kicked can be a real fight stopper and is seldom defended well. The attacker can't find a place to put their feet, blowing their balance and creating openings. Ricochet your foot from stomp to kick and vice versa, gaining energy from the rebound. Switch feet frequently like an Irish jig. It's a United Nations of havoc. It ain't pretty but it works.

1. Ping pong your feet between the ground and target (a low-hanging muay thai heavy bag) simulating stomping toes and smashing shins and insteps. Relax and bounce like a Rockette. You're doing this right when you can hit 3-6 times per second while instantaneously switching feet at will.
2. Add in knee strikes (to the inside and outside of the attacker's thighs).
3. Practice against a partner *without looking at his feet*. You'll find this easy after awhile as you can sense where his feet are while simultaneously delivering hand strikes.

Eye-Gouging: It's What You Need to Do When Your Life Is on the Line

Embarrassingly, there are trained martial artists who think they can stop eye gouges by training their eyelids and facial muscles. The ugly reality is this: *if you drive your finger or thumb straight through the eye socket it has the stopping power of a handgun* (in some cases even more). We're

73

not talking about a scratch, but a *thrust* down past the occipital bone, which can cause convulsions or death. To do this, you need to have the will to do what's necessary, which is why you refrain from violence and any asinine fights if at all possible (Challenge No One).

Simple GCC eye gouging is extremely effective all by itself. In addition, finding the eyes in the midst of a melee is aided by the funnel-shape of the eye socket, which guides the gouge to its target. Some people's natural flinch reaction to eye pokes can make it hard to hit them, however. Ultimate development of the Sensitivity principle within Guided Chaos (parts 2 and 3 of Attack Proof and the associated Companion DVDs) can circumvent this natural flinch reaction altogether. *High-level* sensitivity makes eye gouging totally unstoppable—except to *another* highly trained Guided Chaos practitioner who is trained to defend against them.

Magic Pressure Points

> **BUT WHAT ABOUT ALL THOSE "MAGIC PRESSURE POINTS" I'VE SEEN ON TV?**
>
> **Forget about it.**
>
> You've been watching too many kung fu flicks.
> Or "Kill Bill" reruns.
>
> In real life and death combat there are only two pressure points that really matter: the eyes and the throat. Period. There are others that can cause extreme pain and injury but only these two have guaranteed stopping power. The trick is *getting* to them. As we've said above, GCC will help you do that for 90% of fights. For the other 10% (and for learning how to defend against them) you'll have to learn the more advanced GC.

VIII BASIC STRIKING DRILLS FOR CHAPTERS 9-13

1. The following is a comprehensive list of basic striking drills. Some of them are delivered off of techniques that we haven't mentioned yet but will introduce in the following sections. Come back to this list often and practice them diligently.
2. All of them are essential for developing power and accuracy. We have placed them together for your training convenience.
3. Ideal targets are Muay Thai heavy bags, BOBs or a partner with a kicking shield and/or focus gloves.

1-Slow Jack Benny to chop (the Prow) in air. Do both sides.

2-Full speed screaming Jack Benny to chop (the Prow) on a partner's "drop" cue into air

3-Multiple high speed chops in air on "drop" cue; do both sides

4-Slow Jack Benny to chop (the Prow) followed by palm strike in air using rear cover hand. Do both sides.

5-Full speed screaming Jack Benny to chop (the Prow) followed by palm strike in air with rear cover hand. Do both sides.

6-Slow Jack Benny to chop (the Prow) followed by palm strike and knee in air. Do both sides.

7-Full speed screaming Jack Benny to chop (the Prow) followed by palm strike and knee in air. Do both sides.

8-Same drills as above but against kicking shield/thai pad combo. Can use "drop" as cue or the raising of the hand pad from a horizontal to vertical position (see photos below). Can also use BOB or muay thai bag.

9-Full speed screaming Jack Benny to chop (the Prow) followed by palm strike and knee then multiple screaming palms. Do both sides. Can use "drop" as cue or the raising of the pad from a horizontal to vertical position. *Be sure you have proper form on palms! (Review Middle-linebacker Hitting Drill for what that is.)*

10-ADVANCED: Anywhere Strikes I (p. 37 of Attack Proof). Practice against BOB or heavy bag.

11-ADVANCED: Guided Chaos "Form" p. 90 of Attack Proof 2nd ed.

12-Mexican Hat Dance

13-Slow drop-step kicking in air. Always kick and land to the SIDE of attacker (45 degree angle in). Combine with slow chopping. Also Slow drop-step knee strikes with chops.

14-Stepping off-line low front and round kicks for longer-than-PCZ prelude to Prow or CCUE, performed on low kicking shield. **ALSO perform this drill "on the run" (on the way to escaping).**

Note that the groin should be the target for all kicks, especially if the attacker kicks. The groin is at the enemy's center and is the point of origin for all of *his* kicks. Therefore, if he throws a roundkick, his groin gets hit; if he throws a sidekick, his groin gets hit; if he throws a spinning back kick he gets kicked in the ass. If he throws a front kick it gets intercepted.

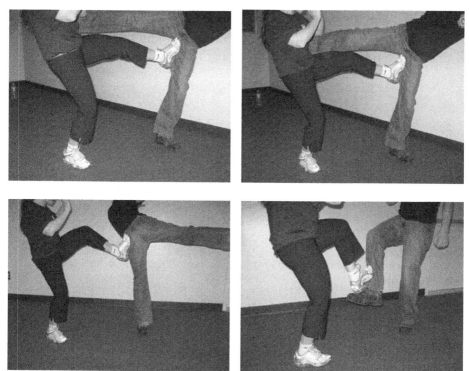

If the enemy throws a sidekick he gets nailed in the 'nads [photo top left]. If he throws a roundkick he gets nailed in the 'nads [photo top right]. A spinning back kick gets it in the butt [photo bottom left]; a front kick, in the shins [photo bottom right].

Sledge hammers on your feet: All of these kicks are made devastatingly more effective by wearing steel-toed footwear which is now available in virtually every style from casual to dress shoe as well as sneakers.

15-Practice "Bowling Ball" eye-gouging methodology on a slowly moving attacker attempting a takedown. Repeat full power on a BOB or similar pad. Practice "following the head." If he moves, elbow smash, rip, find and re-gouge eyes on the "bowling ball."

"Follow the head," rip at eyes while cranking on jaw. Treat eye sockets like bowling ball holes.

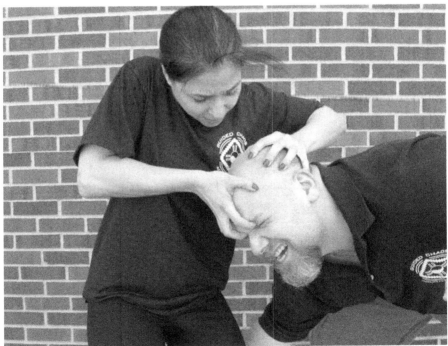

Eye gouging works well with an under-hand rip (like a bowling ball).

16-ADVANCED: Basic chop/palm Rocket-stepping striking drill against BOB or heavy bag. [See Attack Proof 2nd ed. P. 38-39].

Visual action/reaction drill: When the hand shield is suddenly raised, the "victim" strikes instantly out of the Jack Benny with either a chop or a palm/face rip. As per exercise, this can be followed immediately by a palm strike with the other hand and a knee to the kicking shield.

TV Cut Drill (Reaction Speed Training)

THE TV "CUT" DRILL: Essentially you can use the changing pictures on a TV to cue you to hit randomly. By watching fast-paced programming (like MTV or most commercials) *with the sound off* you can develop exceptional visual action-reaction speed better than with almost any other training tool (and it's free!). *Every time the picture "cuts" (changes), throw a strike or series of strikes.* Try it with single strikes, combinations and hand-kick combos in the air and against heavy bags and BOBs. This super high-speed training can easily strain a muscle or tendon SO BE SURE TO WARM UP PROPERLY FIRST!

With the sound OFF, throw a strike or strike combination every time the picture changes. The randomness and pace of music videos and commercials are ideal for this and your reaction speed, balance, Dropping energy and looseness will increase dramatically with regular practice. Make sure to warm up first!

IX THE JACK BENNY/PALM STRIKE-RIP/THE PROW

The "Jack Benny" is a non-threatening "ready" posture from which to strike (Attack Proof p. 14). The "Prow" and the CCUE are the 2 basic GCC Entry Moves with the Prow being the easiest to learn and execute.

[Photo left] The Jack Benny "ready" stance. The "Oh no!" or "Oh my Gosh!" ready stance [photo right]. This lowers the enemy's guard slightly, at which time you drill your fingernails straight through his eye sockets. [See "Courthouse Frenzy" p.43 in Attack Proof 2nd edition.]

— While maintaining your Personal Comfort Zone (PCZ), stand sideways to your aggressor. To reach you, your partner would have to take a step forward.

— Like the old time comedian Jack Benny, touch or stroke your chin with your lead hand as if "contemplating" the words of a suspicious stranger or hostile relation. Keep your elbow down. This non-escalating "ready" stance could alternatively consist of scratching your cheek or head, tugging your hair--essentially anything that provides cover for your neck and face in case of a sudden frontal or rear attack by accomplices. **Quickly scan around for accomplices but snap your attention back instantly to the potential criminal in front of you.** You might also assume a position with *both* hands near your mouth as if saying "oh my God!" This is half way between a regular Jack Benny and a full-on Fright Reaction and allows you to appear scared (which lets his guard down) so that you may be in a position to shoot the fingers of *both* hands into his eyes (see the "elevator attack" in Attack Proof).

81

— Do NOT assume some martial fighting stance, which may only escalate, hasten or provoke an attack. You want to relax the potential attacker and lower *his* guard in case you really do have to take him out.

— **Remember that your PCZ is your trigger.** If he crosses it despite your backing up, you will explode in his face like a grenade.

— Because you've adopted the Jack Benny position, your lead arm is perfectly aligned for a straight shot to the attacker's chin, eyes, or throat while simultaneously deflecting a strike from him (see the "Prow" below for more information on exactly how this works).

THE "PROW"

— From the Jack Benny stance, you attack the attacker by drop-stepping onto the front foot and blasting **either**: 1-a chop to the throat or to the side of the neck; 2-a palm heel/face rip up under the chin to simultaneously crush the vertebra and gouge the eyes (smash on the way in, rip on the way out); 3-a straight spearing stab to the eyes. Experiment to see whether 1,2 or 3 works best for YOU.

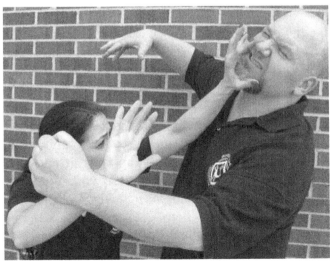

The Prow. Drop step forward and with your lead hand either: smash a palm heel under the chin, chop to the neck, Y-strike to windpipe or spear straight to eyes. Practice each to see which works best for you. Note that the rear hand

82

simultaneously guards against an outside attack. It will *immediately* follow the lead hand into a palm strike (see below).

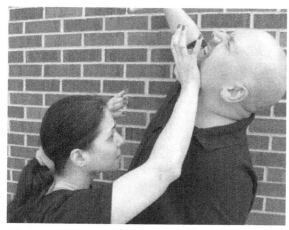

Note that although the *first* position of the arms has the lead hand striking and the rear blocking, this position lasts only a *microsecond* because BOTH hands continue to pummel the enemy like alternating jack hammers afterwards (as in the middle-linebacker hitting drill).

Important Points:

a. The drop-step requires you to drop all your bodyweight straight down on your lead foot as if stomping someone's toes. This should be lightning fast as you bring your rear foot up behind it, kind of a like a quick, compressed fencer's step. The technique is like stomping a fast moving cockroach before it gets away. The front foot is pointed towards the attacker.

b. The rear hand *simultaneously* comes up to protect the face and neck from a side attack (hook punch, etc.)

c. The head is tilted forward and the lead arm's shoulder and elbow held high to act as the "prow" of a boat and deflect an incoming straight punch or jab. The victim should be peering out from behind his lead arm and elbow like Dracula looking over his cape.

d. **As may now be evident, the move is called the "Prow" because the shape of your response acts like the prow of a boat, deflecting water (or in this case, left or right hooks, jabs and crosses) to either side. In other words, you don't block—you deflect as you hit.**

83

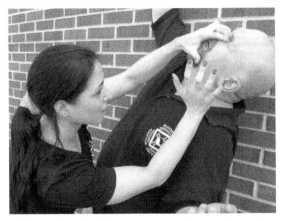

Experiment with both chopping and palm striking/face ripping. Different people with different body types will eventually prefer one to the other. A smaller person with skinny arms might prefer gouging straight to the eyes [below left] because skinny arms are harder to block and have less bone mass for powering an effective chop.

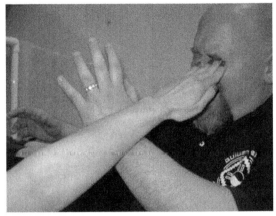

e. The rear cover hand INSTANTLY follows the lead hand with no pause and blasts in with a palm strike/face rip. This is just the first in a barrage of wicked screaming palm strikes delivered either like jackhammers or like the claws of an insane alley cat. Keep your head low and shoulders high to protect your "computer." Your defensive deflection occurs simultaneously because your arms occupy the same entry line your attacker might have used.

---

f. In both Guided Chaos and Guided Chaos Combatives we essentially don't "block" because it wastes time. Your attack *becomes* your defense. Incoming attacks are deflected *on the way to delivering your own* because blocking may cause you to lose the only opportunity or opening you may ever get (right at the beginning of an assault) to stop your attacker.

---

g. In addition, your attacker is probably more powerful than you (which is why he picked you) and would

simply blow through your blocking attempts anyway. If the victim is in a left lead and the attacker left hooks or crosses, the rear cover hand will protect him. If the attacker right hooks, the victim's lead strike will *simultaneously* hit its target first and deflect the attacker's hook. If the attacker throws a straight right it will either be deflected or intercepted. It doesn't matter, because the victim's right palm strike is coming in next anyway.

ADVANCED GC CONCEPT REQUIRING SENSITIVITY:

When *your* initial strike clashes with *his* you can convert his pushing energy on your guard to a pull (yin/yang concept), which greatly augments the power and devastation of your succeeding palm strike with the other hand. Your enemy is effectively pulling himself in to his own destruction. *This is a very simple example of the kind of concepts you can learn in the more advanced Guided Chaos system with its internal energy aspects*

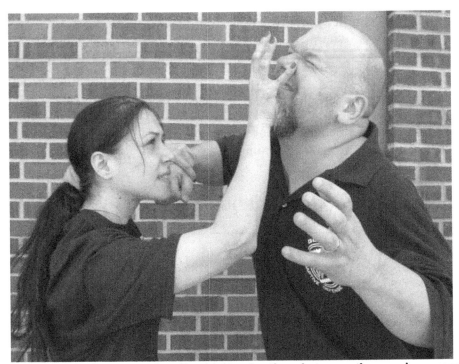

Advanced GC Concept using Sensitivity: In the photo on the previous page, Jeanine's left strike to the enemy's eyes is blocked by his right forearm. Because he is essentially *pushing* on her striking hand, she instantaneously senses the resistance and *reverses his energy by pulling his pushing energy [photo above]*. This feels to the enemy as if his block got sucked down a black hole, as he essentially pushes himself into a right palm to the face, increasing the force with which he is hit with his own energy.

Key Points:
— Stand sideways to the attacker to make a smaller target
— Look unassuming; don't challenge your attacker with an aggressive "fighting" stance.
— Strike from your root
— Do not block
— Strike with all your might
— Strike to kill if you feel like you could die from the assault (if you learn this way from the start you'll be able to back off the energy as necessary. The opposite is *never* true.)
— Cover your face and throat with the rear hand simultaneously
— JACK BENNY/PROW NOTE: For righties we recommend a left lead/chop so that your right hand can access your gun (this also protects the liver). Reverse this for lefties if you carry on your left.

X FRIGHT REACTION SCENARIO DRILLS

We will now combine the striking methodologies into reaction scenarios.

NOTE: it is essential that you have at least 1 training partner to perform these drills. Granted, you can develop your hitting power, speed and timing while practicing solo but you will not get the action/reaction stimulus training you need for your reflex nervous system without having one or more training partners.

Fright Reaction I

1) Get a partner
2) The "victim" stands relaxed with arms at sides and eyes closed.

3) The "attacker" should sneak up and touch the "victim" *lightly* anyplace on the head (including eyelids, ears and tugging the hair). The attacker should be *very* careful to keep his distance when "touching" as what the victim does next could easily cave in his face if the attacker's too close! The idea here is that you want to develop the natural startle or flinch reaction (like

you'd have in an ambush in the dark) into a practical, natural, combative response without any silly, flowery, formalized stances.

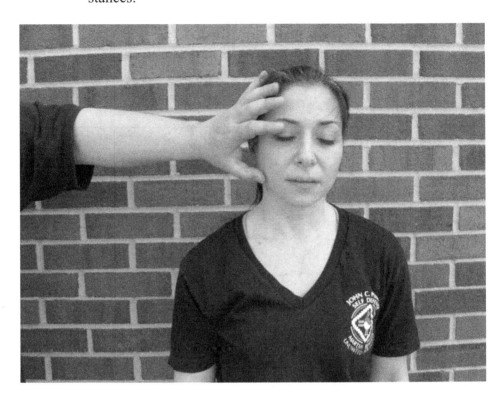

4) This is a focused action/reaction speed drill. As soon as the victim senses the slightest touch **she should open her eyes** and drop explosively into the fright reaction (see next photo). This consists of rapidly bending the knees and lowering the body, widening the stance, raising the shoulders, sinking the head and raising the hands up behind the neck to protect the head and spine. The elbows should be pointing outwards like two spikes that an unwary attacker could become impaled upon. Fingers should NOT be intertwined behind the head to prevent entanglement.

NOTE: this drill is meant for practicing sudden side or rear attacks. Obviously if you're attacked from the front and your eyes are open your response will be different. See the PROW and CCUE (coming up later).

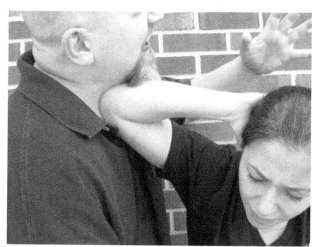

5) The victim should try to increase his/her sensitivity and progressively decrease reaction time. *The fright reaction should be so sudden that the floor shakes (as well as any loose flesh) on dropping.* Recover and repeat starting with step 1.

6) After 20 or 30 repetitions the student should feel very electric, alert and alive as well as balanced, rooted and powerful. Visualize these attributes playing out in a dark alley or anywhere else you could be "surprised."

Fright Reaction II

1) Begin as with 1 and 2 above.
2) The victim should spin several times and then walk, keeping eyes closed.
3) After a few steps, the attacker shoves the victim hard with a padded kicking shield. The shove can come from anywhere against any part of the body (not the face or neck).
4) The victim performs the fright reaction as in 4) above (prior exercise).
5) On the first couple of attempts, the victim will stumble as he attempts to regain his balance. With practice, he will drop and root so explosively and solidly that a *real* "attacker" would get his head smashed in by the victim's elbows snapping into place. (This is without even counter-attacking yet). Eventually, no matter how hard the victim is pushed or from what angle, he/she will land like a great jungle cat.

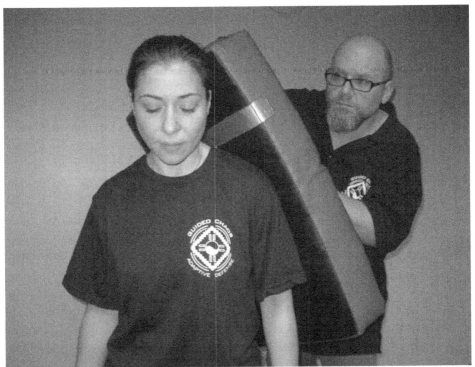

The "victim" rotates with eyes closed until forcefully shoved off balance with a padded kicking shield, at which time she opens her eyes and drops into the Fright

Reaction with lightning speed. The eyes-closed rotation is meant to cause disorientation so the "victim" cannot time their reaction and learns to recover her balance without warning or preparation and in the midst of chaos (or in the dark). Here the enemy sneaks up on Jeanine prior to shoving her so she cannot hear or sense the direction it will come from (for safety while training do NOT shove the "victim" in the head or face).

Fright Reaction III

Have students:
1) Perform steps 1-4 as above.
2) After executing the fright reaction (**do NOT skip this part**), the victim explodes with a barrage of full speed, full power palm strikes/face rips. Make sure they are executed like the Middle-Linebacker Drill (no pushing, pitty-pattying, or foreshortening of limbs).
   a) Step and drive straight into the shield with each strike without pushing. If you push you will be over-committing your balance and will fall if the target moves. **Always rely on your *own* balance and not the target's.**
   b) Smash and rip at the shield as if crushing and snatching cockroaches off a red-hot frying pan without burning your hand. This requires you to pop/drop and ricochet off the target with lightning speed.
   c) Scream on each strike
   d) Always maintain the proper and most powerful hitting range so that you neither over-extend your arms nor cramp them by crowding the target (in Guided Chaos this principle is called "Maintaining Your Sphere of Influence") or standing sideways (which would shorten one arm).
   e) Put your entire body into the strikes by driving from the foot and turning your hips, back and shoulders. **Do not use just arm strength.**
3) Here's the most important part: after 5 or 6 strikes, RUN AWAY!

Fright Reaction IV

Same as III but requires 2 partners, each with his own shield. On a verbal cue (like "Switch!"), the victim attacks the *other* shield. After 2 or 3 switches the victim should run away. DO NOT SKIP THS PART.

After being shoved, opening her eyes and dropping into the Fright Reaction, the "victim" attacks the source of the shove with blood-curdling screams and a vicious barrage of palm heel/face rips, trying to actually tear the leather from the face of the shield on the retraction of each battering strike. On the verbal cue of "Switch!" she turns and attacks the other shield. "Switch!" two or three times and then RUN AWAY! Do *NOT* skip the running away part of the drill.

Key Points:
   — **Learn to drop into the fright reaction instantly**
   — **Attack the attacker from this position**
   — **Never give up fighting**
   — **Practice, practice, practice…**

XI INTERVIEW SCENARIO DRILLS

These essential scenario-based drills use the Personal Comfort Zone to trigger the Jack Benny or similar non-threatening "ready" stances. **They are fundamental to your training because most people do the wrong thing at the wrong time under duress. Train ALL the variations!**

We've already told you that it is next to impossible to defend against an assassination. The interview, however, gives you a short window with which to counter a possible attack from an initially innocuous stranger (or hostile relation) who is checking you out for victimization. Step one was his approaching you unannounced and uninvited. Step two will be his attempt to freeze you in place with eye contact and threatening, charming or even hypnotically engaging conversation. As we repeatedly say, heightened awareness can prevent this by detecting attempted ambushes and by making you look more self-assured--but there are no guarantees.

Regardless of how he got there, the assailant is now directly in front of you. If his words put you on red alert and you feel your adrenaline rising (something you'll learn to respect and channel) or if he crosses the perimeter of your PCZ, **you will strike immediately and keep on striking until you can run.**

As we say repeatedly, no one will blame you for brushing off and running from *any* stranger's words but this can lead to a state of perpetual paranoia which is not healthy and cannot be maintained. You can just make it your general policy to never stop and talk to strangers *ever*. You just say "sorry, no time" and keep walking, but keep your eyes on him and on your surroundings for potential accomplices.

However, because you may sometimes be cornered or otherwise unable to leave, or *you may want to respond to a questionable person's entreaties in certain situations*, you need to learn a "heightened readiness" maneuver that gets you ready to protect yourself if necessary. Instead of going straight into a Fright Reaction, you adopt a non-threatening position with your lead hand stroking your chin (like the old comic Jack Benny) or a similar contemplative or nervous position (touching/scratching your face, hair, etc. with one or both hands) while standing sideways to the stranger and maintaining your PCZ. **You should also instantly begin looking** around for accomplices the moment a stranger begins talking to you-- but always snap your attention back to the interviewer. By the way, if you stand assertively and all puffed up you may actually *provoke* an attack that might not have occurred otherwise. Remember, he already picked you out. Unless you're a professional actor who's perfected the "foaming at the mouth" routine, it's better now to appear *weaker* to encourage him to let his guard down. Again, he's *already* selected you as his victim.

The Interview Variations Drill trains your awareness and maintenance of your PCZ, scanning for accomplices, moving offline, and differentiating between idiotic confrontations and REAL danger. The purpose of these strategies is to give the scumbag every opportunity to change his mind. If you keep *giving* space and he keeps *taking* it, he will cross your PCZ and now be within your Sphere of Influence (the totality of your weaponry). Entering this zone acts as your trigger. He has now voided any rights of safety and you have no more moral ambiguity about what needs to be done. You will explode into him like a grenade.

Be sure to train ALL the interview variations described below. For maximum benefit, this requires the "Interviewer" to practice all the variations as well. Begin each Interview Variation with the following two steps:

1) Get yourself a partner and have him hold a "focus glove" (boxing/martial art accessory) that has two eyes drawn on it—or a hockey mask taped to it to mimic the enemy's face and eye sockets [see photo below].
2) With your eyes closed, spin around 3 times (to create disorientation) and then start walking, keeping your eyes closed until you are addressed.

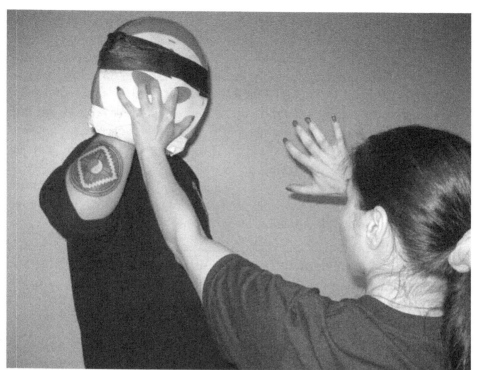

Gouge "Jason" in the eyes: a hockey mask taped to a focus glove makes a great target. Do not hold the focus glove too close to your face or you could wind up eating it like Joe just did!

INTERVIEW SCENARIO VARIATIONS (be sure to practice ALL of them):

1) The instant your partner begins the "interview" by talking to you, open your eyes. Immediately scan for accomplices, assert your PCZ, keep moving and get your hands into the Jack Benny or similar dissuasive "ready" stance. **(You should have a 2nd "attacker" positioned behind the victim to remind him to scan around by touching or *gently* feigning a "strangling" rear assault.)**

2) If your partner says, "Come with me", "Get in the car," **or presents a gun or a knife** (use fakes), **run away** *immediately*. Practice each sub-variation. Note that you're not being restrained in this scenario and the attacker is not right on top of you. It is *threat* response we're drilling here.

3) "NOT INTERESTED" VARIATION: If your partner starts with some seemingly innocuous chatter like, "You got change?" "You

95

got the time?" or "How do you get to . . .?" say "no" and keep on walking but be alert for a rear or side attack from the assailant or an accomplice. Keep your hands up in an "I'm not interested" position to prevent a rear choke attack lock down on your throat.

4) "INTERESTED" VARIATION: If your partner says something that seems totally safe and you're interested, stick around and talk to the "stranger" but immediately adopt the Jack Benny anyway and remember to maintain your PCZ. It is ESSENTIAL to train BOTH variations 3 and 4.

5) If when you open your eyes you see that a wall, furniture, or other objects trap you, then immediately adopt the Jack Benny stance and back away slowly as far as you can.

Giving space is important to justify what is to follow. Be aware that scam artists, kidnappers, rapists or serial killers will often address you with reassuring conversation to get your guard down.

---

6) If after your partner starts talking to you he reaches for or strikes at you, react as follows: Since he entered your PCZ, attack the attacker with the Prow, using your partner's focus glove as the target. Drop-step forward and strike with your lead hand, using a palm heel/face rip, Y Strike to the throat, spear hand to the eyes or a chop to the front or side of the "throat" (on the *focus glove*, not on your partner). Both of your hands come out *simultaneously*, with the closer one hitting first. The rear hand acts as protection against the attacker's potential strikes. **(In real life, if someone physically enters your personal comfort zone under these circumstances, attack the attacker right now with everything you've got.)** Instantly follow by slamming the glove with palm heels and tearing into the "eyes". Scream like a Banshee. Drive with your legs and pump your arms like jackhammers. Visualize tearing the attacker's face off and try actually ripping the leather from the skin of the glove. Hit 5 to 10 times and then run away (do NOT skip this part). In keeping with the Prow principles, your partner's other hand, if reaching for you, will be deflected incidentally by your arms as you go straight toward your target, like the prow of a boat splitting water to either side. Do not block. The shape of your strikes creates your defense.

Advanced Restraint Variation Scenarios with Weapons

7) If, when your partner addresses you, he is **right on top of you** while demanding money **"NOW!"** **and brandishing or announcing he has a gun or knife,** say "OK, you got me, you're the boss" etc., and give him your whole wallet/purse, or place it on the ground, depending on his instructions. The "attacker" should then leave. Note that mounting a defense in this scenario is probably not only unnecessary, it exposes you to greater danger due to his weaponry and proximity to lethal targets. Don't fight if you don't have to.

The following variations are the trickiest. So far, this manual has provided simple defenses that are easy to learn and practice. We will outline *basic* weapons responses here but take heed that comprehensive defenses involve many critical parameters and are beyond the scope of this manual. For this reason, we strongly recommend studying the Weapons chapters in Attack Proof 2nd edition and the Guided Chaos Bare Hands to Hand Guns DVD.

---

8) Same as 7 but after he has your money he says, "Come with me!" or "Get in the van!" This is the moment of truth. You do NOT want to go to Crime Scene #2. You will have to Attack the Attacker but WHEN and HOW are tricky because you are being restrained (perhaps with a gun barrel jammed in your mouth and a forearm crushing your throat). This is where you would need to apply the advanced weapon defenses in Attack Proof and especially the Bare Hands to Hand Guns DVD. This is because slight changes in angle and weapon presentation dictate different defenses that are much easier to learn from video without lengthy written descriptions that could be *misinterpreted* or *misapplied.*

Understand that we don't want to be cavalier about this. *Gun and knife defenses are different from hand-to-hand and anyone who tells you that they have one technique for every gun or knife attack has no idea what they're talking about.* For example, clearing (or disarming) the gun or knife as you strike is dependent upon the precise location of the weapon in relation to critical centerlines on your head or torso. In addition, **certain restraint postures are next to impossible to defend against and you can die trying.** In these scenarios it is vital to *get the attacker to change his hold on you while attempting to move you to a more secure location.* **For the purposes of this manual, we simply want to say that you should begin to practice your acting routines because there may be no other way to accomplish this.** Your subterfuge can include faking chest pains, weak knees, feinting, shortness of breath, fear paralysis, etc., anything that makes it difficult to restrain and move you simultaneously in his current configuration. For example, you could say, "Please…please…uhhh…" etc., while your knees begin to buckle. The instant he changes his grip, you explode into him. This may be your only chance so you want to practice these acting routines regularly. Considering the stress of an assault, the reality of your fear may not be too far from the truth but at least you will be trained in the response. The Fear Meditation explained earlier in this manual is helpful. You have to assume that no one will come to your rescue. *Inaction* could prove fatal.

Key Points:
— **The first strike is merely the first in a series of snarling, slashing, crushing blows**
— **In general, as initial strikes, chin jabs and eye gouges work better for smaller individuals than throat chops**
— **Train yourself mentally to spear right through the eye sockets**
— **KEY POINT: AVOID THE SPARRING MENTALITY. If someone wants to "fight" and dances around, back away. Remember, if *he* backs up, *you* back up. If he then charges, drop-step kick into him.**

XII CLOSE COMBAT UNIVERSAL ENTRY (C.C.U.E.)

The Prow and the CCUE are both entry methods, with the CCUE being more effective (but slightly more complicated to execute). The CCUE also provides more safety because instead of diving right into the attack and "splitting" it, you step in but slightly off-line. Learn the Prow first and then experiment with the CCUE.

A critical flaw of most systems of self-defense is that they force you to learn different responses to both left and right-sided attacks, i.e. "if he attacks me with a left hook I respond with a right block but if he attacks with a *right* hook I counter with a *left* block." This is insanity. The human brain (especially under duress) cannot anticipate or respond quickly or accurately enough to pick between the two defenses on demand. Now multiply your required defense options by other multi-directional assault variations such as jabs, crosses, uppercuts, overheads, bum rushes, grabs, kicks and takedowns and it becomes overwhelming. Despite what you may have seen in movies, television and the dojo, the odds of a successful "calculated" instantaneous response become nil.

Criminal Assault vs. Sparring:

1-In a *real* attack, the enemy will come directly at you from where ever he is

2-If he attacks *indirectly* with side steps, feints, jives, etc., this is some ego-based sparring or fighting scenario and not an actual criminal assault on your life. Leave the area, keeping an eye on him.

3-If *he* steps back, *you* step back. This has become a cock-fight and not an actual criminal assault. Again, leave the area but be vigilant for accomplices. Later, you will need to think hard about how you got mixed up in such an idiotic situation in the first place.

4-If he then rushes in, drop-step in and slightly off-line and kick directly at the groin or shins followed by either the Prow, CCUE, or multiple gouging palm heel strikes.

As shown earlier, the straight groin kick works as a kicking defense no matter what kind of kick the attacker throws (round, side or spinning) because your target is his kick's point of origin: the mid-pelvis or groin.

99

The CCUE

As described above, if an attack is for real, the enemy will cross your Personal Comfort Zone and come right at you. In order to throw a monkey wrench into his attack, the most important thing to do is to step off-line and *in* at a 45 degree angle. Stepping back or directly to the side just gives him room to regroup and re-launch his attack. Also, stepping back as a close-range fighting defense puts you at a tactical advantage from which you may never recover because you will be run down (note this is not the same as a quick drop step back from which you explode forwards--an advanced technique).

Here are the 4 basic moves of the CCUE that need to be performed simultaneously:

1-Step offline and in at a 45 degree angle in the direction that feels most natural to you. Typically for a righty using a left lead this will be to the right with your right foot. Experiment with both sides. **Find out which side feels stronger and faster** *and then use that direction exclusively against any attack regardless of whether it's left or right. This is the key concept of the CCUE.* We will explain why in a moment.
2-Intercept and clear the incoming attack
3-Attack the attacker with a chop to the throat or neck
4-Follow up instantly with a palm heel/eye rip
NOTE: For righties we recommend moving right with a left chop so that your right hand can access your gun after the left chop (this also protects the liver). Reverse this for lefties if you carry on your left.

Presuming you started with a left lead Jack Benny and stepped in with your right foot, your right hand will come sweeping down and in from upper right to lower left, smashing the incoming strike out of the way with a splashing (not pushing) motion, while your left hand shoots in, in a circular motion simultaneously from wherever it is to where your right hand was an instant earlier (up and outside to the right and above the path of the right arm) and then slashes down and inside to the left like an ax with a chop to the attacker's neck or spine. This is immediately followed by a palm heel to the temple with the other hand (the one that did the clearing motion). Note that the combined motion resembles a swimming side-stroke.

The CCUE step-by-step (Note: 1 and 2 actually happen simultaneously, we are only breaking them down to explain them): 1- Step forward at a 45 degree angle with your rear foot (beginner) or front foot (advanced) and simultaneously clear an incoming strike with the rear hand with a drop "splashing" motion.

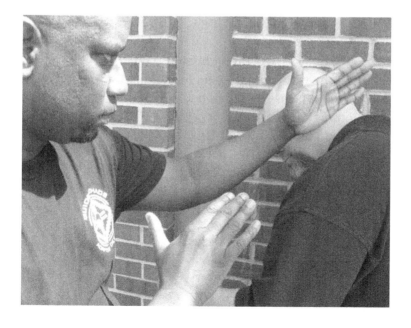

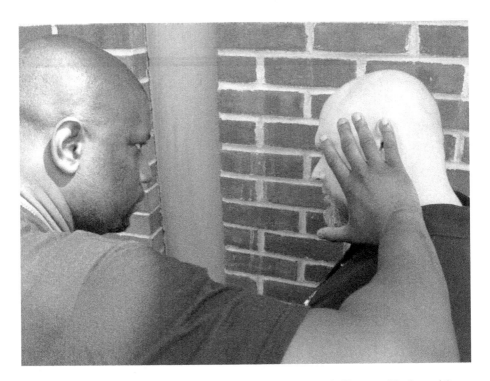

[PHOTO 2. bottom previous page]-Slash down on the neck like a guillotine with a dropping chop strike.
[PHOTO 3 above]-Follow with a palm strike and knee (Note: the knee may precede the palm depending on which foot makes the initial step).

As noted above, the core principle of this entry is its universality:

--If the attacker jabs or crosses with his left, your right clearing hand will "splash" it out of the way, providing an entry route for the left chop.
--If the attacker right jabs, crosses or hooks, your entry is simpler because there will be nothing in your way.
-- If the attacker left hooks you will find that because your clearing motion is foreshortened you will easily check the hook because your right hand will be caught moving to the outside right (inside of the hook). Simultaneously, your left chop will come down on his neck like an ax, completely unimpeded.

An incoming left jab gets cleared [photo above left]. An incoming right cross or hook leaves him totally open [photo above right].

In the photo on the left, if he throws a left hook, the defender's foreshortened clearing move with his right hand naturally becomes a check with no change in motion. Photo on the right shows how a foreshortened CCUE turns into a Fright Reaction.

No matter what the enemy attacks you with, the CCUE response is the same because you are moving off-line of a direct attack. It works even if your awareness is down and the attacker jumps your space too quickly to mount a full CCUE [photo bottom right]. In this case, the foreshortened CCUE becomes an ordinary fright reaction. The attacker winds up eating an elbow straight to the face, followed by chops and palms. Here, a right chop would unfold out of the right elbow, followed by a left palm/face rip.

The last automatic move in the CCUE sequence is a knee strike, which naturally flows off the clear and chop. It usually comes before the palm but sometimes is simultaneous or after depending on your stepping and delivery. The more advanced method of stepping with the CCUE (which requires more precise timing and distance) uses the *lead* foot to step in obliquely to the right. This is actually quicker but the angle of entry is narrower with fewer margins for error.

STOPPING A TAKEDOWN WITH THE CCUE

The knee strike stops a takedown cold by caving in the head of the attacker regardless of whether he dives in for either leg or both. Since you're doing it along with the hand strikes *regardless of the type of attack* it presents an effective high/low defense and will either crush his thigh muscle in a high-line assault or crack his head or neck in a surprise low take down attempt. On the latter, the clearing motion or chop transforms into a palm heel to the head or neck or a spearing elbow to the spine. This is delivered convulsively with the knee and elbow acting like a pincer.

In the photo on the left, after the elbow strike, the defender will immediately go to an under-handed bowling ball gouge, rip and neck break using the eye-sockets as bowling ball holes. Yes it's savage, but you didn't ask for this fight, you did your best to avoid it. Right?

ADDITIONAL BASIC STRIKING DRILLS

The following are the basic strikes contained within the CCUE, including the front kick (which can be the prelude to the CCUE when attacking the attacker from just outside of or at the edge of your PCZ). When practicing them, whether on a heavy bag or with a partner, start off ultra-slow, working up to full speed, while controlling your balance and working within your Sphere of Influence.

Note – all of this can be done against a Muay Thai heavy bag if you're working alone, or with a partner holding a striking shield. The best target combination, if available, is a kicking shield held in one hand and a Muay Thai pad stacked above it in the other hand. The shield is for the knee strikes and kicks while the Thai pad is for the chop/palm combinations.

The 12 Step Striking Entry Drill

1. Side chop moving forwards (to the throat)

2. Side chop, palm heel (to the face) moving forwards

3. Side chop, palm heel, knee strike moving forwards

4. Side chop, palm heel, knee strike, elbow strike (to the neck) moving forwards

5. Clear with your right hand (CCUE) while stepping off line to the right at a 45°degree angle and strike with a left side chop (to the neck)

6. Clear with your right hand (CCUE) while stepping off line to the right at a 45°degree angle and strike with a left side chop (to the neck) and left knee strike

7. Clear with your right hand (CCUE) while stepping off line to the right at a 45°degree angle and strike with a left side chop (to the neck) and left front kick to the near side leg. Now do 5-7 stepping off-line to the left with a right chop, right knee and right kick.

8. Left front low kick and left front chop moving forward. Right front low kick and right front chop moving forward.

9. Left front kick to right palm heel moving forward. Right front kick to left palm heel moving forward

10. Left front kick, right hand clear/left side chop (CCUE), right palm heel, moving forward

11. Left front kick, right hand clear/left side chop (CCUE), right palm heel, right knee strike, moving forward (try also the knee *before* the palm strike)

12. Left front kick, right hand clear/left side chop (CCUE), right palm heel, right knee strike, moving forward (try also the knee *before* the palm strike), left elbow strike moving forward. Try 9-12 starting with the opposite hand/foot.

Key Points:
— Warm up with the basic strikes shown above
— Start slow and then build up speed
— Strike to cut the pads and not push them
— Keep the hands up
— Keep the arms bent when striking

Ensure that as you enter with the upper body strikes your striking elbow or arm is high enough to protect your throat and face. This position is called "The Drac" because of its resemblance to Count Dracula peeking out from behind his cape. Ensure that your other hand is up to also protect the throat.

"The Drac." Your elbow protects your face and throat. If the enemy jumps your space, they become impaled on the point, as with the Fright Reaction. The chop whips out at any time to the enemy's windpipe.

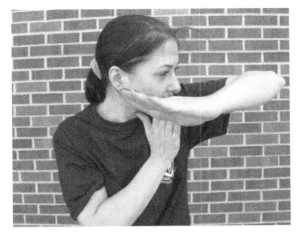

"The Drac" [side view]

— Launch from your root, control your Sphere of Influence, maintain balance and do not lean
— Hit with full dropping energy against kicking shields, muay thai heavy bags and BOBs (do not kick the base of a BOB or you'll have a mess on your hands!)
— End it as quickly as possible
— Strike naturally, strike to kill. Remember the "Baseball Bat" Analogy. You fight ONLY to save your life or a loved one's, not to defend your ego, honor or reputation.
— Experiment with using the CCUE and the Prow in the Interview Drills. See which works better for you.

XIII THE BOX STEP, MULTIPLE ATTACKERS AND SIMPLIFIED GROUNDFIGHTING

> **The Box Step constitutes the last part of Guided Chaos Combatives and forms the "bridge" to the far more advanced Guided Chaos.**

The box step teaches you to move smoothly like a cat, perfectly balanced and in complete control of your body's entire mass and equilibrium as you step to new root points around or even behind your attackers. You will evade strikes while staying close to dish out the most mayhem. This becomes especially important in Guided Chaos when you begin training Sensitivity and Adaptability to any movement and situation. *You need to do this without leaning, hopping, crossing, twisting or sliding your feet or leaving your rear foot mired in place like it was nailed there (a fault of many classic stances).*

The end result is that you will be ready and able to deliver a strike from any position in relation to the enemy. Most importantly, it will teach you to move with full **Body Unity** (a Guided Chaos principle) that you can channel into any weapon. This is vital against multiple attackers in the dark, as you can read about in the real life story *The Williams Brothers' Attack* in Attack Proof.

1. Mark out a box on the ground, roughly 3 feet by 3 feet
2. Stand in an L-shaped stance, with the heel of your right (forward) foot in one corner of the box and the left (rear) foot behind it and outside the box at about a 90-degree angle to the right foot.
3. From there, step with your rear foot clockwise to another corner of the box, landing in an L but now with your *left* foot forward. **Do this *without* twisting the front foot prior to take off.**
4. Continue stepping to a new corner with your rear foot, which, when it lands, becomes the new forward foot. You always step in the direction of the rear foot. If your right foot is forward, stepping with your rear (left) foot to the corner on your left is the easiest (a 90 degree box step). A little tougher is stepping with your rear foot to the corner directly across the box. This requires you to turn 180 degrees in the air clockwise and land facing in the direction from which you came. Most difficult is bringing your rear (left) foot all the way to the corner of the box directly to your right. This means you have to turn your body 270 degrees in the air

clockwise. With all these movements, you never cross your feet, and you never step behind yourself.

5. Continue to do this drill back and forth in both directions, stepping to any corner at random without pause.

> If you feel your weight is off when you land, you are off balance, and you need to adjust in the air. This will present a challenge with the more difficult steps. **To get your feet to land properly without twisting, you will have to get your hips moving early while you're still in the air.**

Keep in mind the importance of **how** you step:

• When you step to your new position, don't hop or jump. Glide softly and smoothly, like a cat hugging the ground (or like Groucho Marx). **Do not twist either foot, either on take off or landing.**

• Rise as little as possible, as if at the apex of your step you might hit your head on a very low ceiling.

• Be careful not to lean too far back or too far forward when landing in your new position.

• **When you land, be sure your feet are in the final L-stance before each makes contact with the ground so you don't have to readjust or twist either foot in any way.**

• Land the new front foot smack in the middle of the new corner.

Perform the box drill, but each time you land, throw a strike. This drill trains you to land balanced and ready to throw a strike, and then immediately go into the next box step.

1. Begin with low kicks, such as short front kicks, roundhouses, sidekicks, knee kicks, whatever. The type of kick is not important.

2. Try the kicks using either your front or rear leg as soon as you land. This will require you to be in the dead center of your equilibrium; otherwise you'll lean, fall, and have no power.

3. If you do this drill with a few partners, each of them can be positioned outside a corner of the box with his or her own kicking shield, which you will kick after each box step. Your partners will step in toward you from the opposite corners with their shields.

4. Try this using upper body strikes. Remember, the type of strike is unimportant, but you should try everything you can think of.

5. Try this exercise holding light weights or a baseball bat. Using a sledgehammer is a real challenge.[see the advanced Battle-axe Box Step in Attack Proof 2nd ed.]

The Box Step starting position. In the photo above, note the 4 corners of the box marked on the floor (Joe is standing on one of them). From here, Joe will box step with his rear (left) foot to the corner on his left so that his left foot becomes the new front foot. The feet must always start and end right smack in the middle of the corner. It is absolutely imperative in all the steps that THE FEET NEVER TWIST, either in preparation for take-off or on landing.

 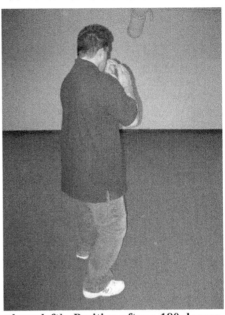

Position after a 90 degree Box Step [photo above left]. Position after a 180 degree Box Step [photo above right].

Position after a 270 degree ("Baryshnikov") Box Step. Joe has landed dead center in his corner after completing a smooth, gliding, step/jump/spin to his left. This requires rapid, pronounced hip rotation and excellent balance so that you land surely and stealthily like a jungle cat without even a millimeter of foot twist. If your foot moves even slightly you're wasting your time.

Add kicking with either your front or rear foot the INSTANT you land with no foot position adjustment whatsoever.

APPLYING THE BOX STEP TO MULTIPLE ATTACKERS

Although this subject is more completely addressed within Guided Chaos (because of important Sensitivity, Looseness and Adaptability principles), the Box Step will make a GCC defense extremely devastating all by itself.

The box step teaches you to move smoothly like a cat, perfectly balanced and in complete control of your body's entire mass and equilibrium as you step to new root points around or even behind your attackers.

1-**The first step in dealing with multiple attackers is avoidance.** As explained earlier, give all loitering gangs a wide berth. Don't expect an assertive or confident attitude, nor being able to "speak their language" to protect you.

2- If they're beginning to close in but an attack is not definite, DO NOT STAND STILL. This makes you a sitting duck. Keep moving, looking around and talking with your hands as you assume a dynamic Jack Benny type position. DO NOT remain in a motionless stance.

3-If they're already in your face and the threat is imminent, Attack the Attacker: strike straight to the eyes of the nearest gang member using the Prow or CCUE.

4-Using the Box Step, circle behind the first member you hit. **Keep him *between* you and the next attacker.**

> **Never fight between two people. Continuously Box-step to keep the person you're hitting between you and the next person.**

5-Strike like a sewing machine with chops to the neck and throat, palm heels to the head and spear hands to the eyes. **Never back up: keep box stepping, hitting and circling or you will be tackled and thrown to the ground, which is a whole 'nother world. As you step and strike (but *not* while you Box Step), stomp the ground (Mexican Hat Dance) to crush toes. This augments your balance and makes it difficult for anyone to grab your legs.** Knock the heads of your attackers together like coconuts when possible and use the nearer person's body as a shield against the person behind him, BUT DO THIS WITH MOTION AND STRIKING, **NOT** WITH GRABBING, GRAPPLING OR LOCKING. You can rip and tear at eye sockets, hair, loose flesh, etc. **not fixate or hold anywhere with grabs on the attackers' bodies.** This immobilizes you and again, makes you a sitting duck.

6- As soon as there's an opening, break out of the circle and run.

7- **DO NOT GRAPPLE.** If you tie up with one person **YOU ARE FINISHED** as they will then all pile on and kick your head in. If you lose your balance or are thrown to the ground you will need to use Guided Chaos Groundfighting, which is basically modified Native American "anything goes" kicks, spins and rolls all performed on the move from the ground. This is a whole methodology that is beyond the scope of this manual but involves moving your body like a live fish on a frying pan or a break dancer to keep your head away from the attackers' boots and your feet between them and you as you deliver side, round, hook and mule kicks, all while spinning on the ground. *This is done only until you can get up and run.* This type of kicking can be practiced from the ground against

114

low hanging heavy bags or kicking shields. For the complete methodology, drills and strikes, read the Groundfighting chapter in Attack Proof 2nd edition or see our Guided Chaos Groundfighting DVD available at attackproof.com.

8- Look for makeshift weapons in your environment you can grab quickly as you are spinning (rocks, pipes, sticks, bottles). Even a stout metal pen can be held in an ice pick grip and used as a stabbing weapon.

If you have a knife or gun, Box stepping will give you the time and space to access it. This is why Police officers need proper hand-to-hand training: criminals may strip them of their weapons and use them against them. Weapons fighting is a complete methodology on its own that is beyond the scope of this manual. If you are interested there is an entire DVD Weapons Series available (Gun, Knife and Cane) at attackproof.com.

Cultivate and maintain a kill-or-get-killed mindset: you will need it to survive a fight with multiple attackers. If you diligently practice all the material in this manual your odds of going home to your family alive are far higher than with sportive, flowery or classical methods of martial arts. Practice the Focus Your Fear meditation and harness that energy when hitting the BOB, heavy bags and kicking shields. Hit them loosely but as fast and hard as you can with full Dropping Energy and penetrate them like a drill. Box step around a swinging bag or partners with shields. Try to RIP the leather from the bags. This will serve you well when you have to crush the scrotums and tear the faces off your attackers and use their eye sockets like bowling ball holes. No games here, no rules. This is your *life* we're talking about and *this* is how you save it.

FIGHTING ON THE GROUND

Despite everything, you may wind up on the ground. Take it from real war combat veterans and cops who've survived real bloody melees: **Do NOT try to emulate the sportive grappling you see on TV or in dojos if you want to LIVE.** These are competitive bouts between almost super-human, star athletes who are nevertheless protected by RULES. Their goal is to WIN. Yours is to SURVIVE. To quote Professor Brad Steiner, President of the International Combat Martial Arts Federation:

"A choice must be made. If a method can be practiced full force in a competitive venue, then obviously it lacks crippling, maiming, and killing skills — all of which, whether it is popular to say so or not, must be taught and embedded in the student's psyche and nervous system. If a system is fully combat worthy, then any competition or full contact training in the skills (except against dummies and other insentient training aids) is nothing short of insanity."

IF YOU FALL OR ARE THROWN TO THE GROUND, keep moving and rolling to keep your head away from their boots and kick their shins by swinging and

thrusting your legs using body inertia. By presenting only *your* boots and legs to a knife while smashing *their* legs, you reduce stabs and cuts to your vital organs and head (this also may give you the only opportunity of time and space to access your *own* knife or gun). Get up and run as soon as possible.

DO NOT GRAPPLE. Destroy and keep moving. Rip eyes, throat, crush testicles; bite any available flesh. The power you can generate from swinging ground kicks (like break dancing) is enormous. In the photo on the bottom of the previous page, note the scissoring heel kick to the back. These kicks are extremely dangerous; take great care practicing against live partners. Use full power against low hanging muay thai heavy bags or kicking shields. Practice high-speed evasion rolling (horizontally like a log in addition to tumbling) between partners or 2 or 3 heavy bags while delivering kicks. Practice getting to your feet and running.

In the photo above, note the knee to the face and the axe kick preparing to crash down on his skull. You can also do thrusting mule kicks with one or both legs with your palms on the ground. Practice rolling out of this position and kicking from your side to avoid being pinned on your stomach.

Consider the fighting methodology of a wild alley cat that's off its feet: you have to deal with its rear legs raking your flesh, mixed with occasional rips from the front legs and penetrating bites. You can't even get to its body. It writhes and twists like rubber to avoid being pinned while simultaneously biting and kicking with clawed feet. *You* don't have claws on your feet but you *do* have shoes (hopefully steel-toed) that effectively give you sledgehammers at the end of each leg, something a cat *doesn't* have. You also have hand grip strength and dexterity a cat doesn't have for tearing, twisting and snapping.

But again, don't grapple—it will only immobilize you. Snap and go. You will never see a wildcat grapple, lock, or otherwise tie-up with an enemy. It penetrates and destroys and then runs. For more information, the entire Guided Chaos Groundfighting training regimen can be found in Attack Proof 2nd edition and the GC Groundfighting DVD on attackproof.com.

Practice everything in this manual and the odds of your surviving violent crime will improve exponentially. Even if all you do is practice the Awareness Strategies in Chapter 1, you minimize your exposure to bad things happening in the first place, which crime statistics show is even MORE important than self-defense. If the shit hits the fan, fight with everything you've got, don't give up and you will likely see your family again.

XIV LEGAL RAMIFICATIONS

Self-defense--AFTER you've defended yourself: What the law says about self-protection, and what to do after the threat has passed.

Your "Rights" As a Victim

Let's compare what a police officer can and cannot do when his life is in danger versus what a civilian can do. Cops are in a Catch-22 twilight zone as far as their personal safety goes because virtually any situation they respond to could turn into a bloodbath. They never know if a given suspect will be cooperative, remain so, or explode into violence--with or without a hidden weapon. Add to this the fact that any ne'er-do-well who resists or challenges a cop is basically a psycho anyway. What normal person takes on a uniformed officer carrying mace, baton and sidearm thinking it will end well for him?

Ironically, the officer's dilemma is further compounded because they are obligated by law to follow strict (yet often contradictory) rules of engagement that tend towards the politically correct. Tactics and mountains of paperwork are designed to prevent "brutality" lawsuits brought by criminals against their captors. This translates into standardized training that includes locks, hold and other less-than-lethal submission techniques that have been proven to be less-than-ideal, cumbersome and dangerous because their stopping power is severely limited. This is why on COPS and other TV reality shows you often see the men in blue "pile on." It takes several officers to subdue a perp and prevent excessive injury. The reality is that backup isn't always available and the over-handicapped and now desperate cop may need to resort prematurely to his sidearm because he didn't have the hand-to-hand skills to subdue the criminal. It all comes with the job because the cop must actively *seek out* criminality to arrest it.

In contrast, the civilian is typically minding his own business and should be (if he's smart) *avoiding* all conflicts and violent scenarios. Nevertheless, if the civilian is assaulted and his life is in danger, he is, depending on state and local laws, under no such obligations as the police officer. In many courtrooms he will not be convicted for having to use force, up to and including lethal force, to survive. But there are no guarantees. As they say, "I'd rather be judged by 12 than carried by 6."

And as far as police tactics go, we're not going to get into a lengthy argument over local laws, department policies, politics, and civil rights but suffice it to say that geared down "lethal-force" training tends to be safer not only for the police officer but for the perpetrator as well. As we say above, a cop who can't fight is far more likely to use his gun.

Key Points to remember *after* fighting for your life:
— DO NOT, DO NOT, DO NOT speak with the police!
— Kindly tell them to speak to your lawyer
— No matter how much they try to convince you that they're just trying to help, do not talk to them.
— If you speak with the police, no matter how justified you feel you were, even if you were 100% correct in defense of your life, YOU *WILL* BE CHARGED!!!
— ONCE AGAIN: DO NOT, DO NOT, DO NOT speak with the police!
— So, as you are reading this manual, the time to go find yourself a competent attorney is RIGHT NOW, not after the shit hits the fan. Start asking for referrals TODAY.
— IMPORTANT: If the stress of the attack has left you with unusual chest pains, do NOT ignore these life-threatening signs (not to mention any other injuries). Ask for an ambulance immediately.
— Other key points to remember:

Do's	Don'ts
▪ Avoid all fights ▪ Run if you can ▪ Keep the majority of your strikes above the shoulder ▪ Strike to the neck from every angle ▪ Strike with all of your might and strike to penetrate ▪ Strike to kill, never strike to wound if you feel you're	▪ Do not attempt to grapple or control people--it will only slow you down. If someone grabs you, strike them in the eyes or the throat ▪ Do not go to the ground and grapple with an attacker. If you fall to the ground, strike and kick with all of your might and

- going to die (remember the baseball bat analogy)
- Maintain an outward focus; be especially receptive to sudden movement
- Control you sphere of influence or personal zone
- Always be prepared to step off line
- Always be prepared to go into action and use deadly force
- Think about what you want to do in the event of an ambush, kidnapping attempt etc... develop your battle drill, practice, practice, practice. Then "what if" every possible scenario you can think of and repeat the steps above
- Expect the Unexpected
- Never, ever give up fighting

- get to your feet as quickly as possible
- Never let them get the drop on you and never drop your guard
- Do not allow people to encroach on your space
- Do not allow yourself to be cornered or boxed in
- Never ever allow yourself to be moved from one location to another, it's always better for them and worse for you
- Do not ever assume the enemy will behave in a predictable manner, the enemy will always do what he wants

XV SELECTED READINGS

> *COMING SOON:*
> GUIDED CHAOS COMBATIVES VIDEO DOWNLOADS
> **AVAILABLE AT WWW.ATTACKPROOF.COM**

Selected Readings for Warrior Mindset Development

Below are what we believe to be minimum required readings one should undertake in order to gain a full appreciation of the proper mindset for effective fighting skills. While there are other great books out there we feel this list of books provides the clearest and most concise understanding of the proper mindset needed to develop an effective self defense posture. We call these the "Canons of Warrior Mindset Development."

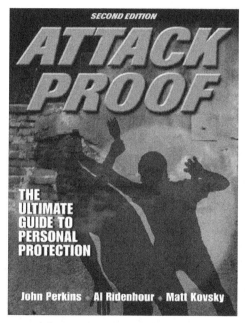

Attack Proof: The Ultimate Guide to Personal Protection 2nd Edition, Perkins, et. al., Human Kinetics, (2009)
Revolutionary in its presentation, Attack Proof explains a system of *Adaptive Defense* that acknowledges that all real violence is unchoreographed chaos, thus rendering ordinary technique-based training useless.

Former forensic crime scene expert John Perkin's art of Guided Chaos eliminates all patterned techniques, allowing a practitioner to create his defense spontaneously. It is the true link between the internal energy concepts of tai chi and the nuts and bolts killing efficiency of World War II Close Quarters Combat. Guided Chaos Combatives (modified WW II CQC) provides the elementary weaponry and is the first part of Guided Chaos.

"Attack Proof" lays the foundation for developing the proper mindset for combat along with the skills necessary to deal with wanton violence. At this stage of the game, without "Attack Proof," many of the other books would lack the proper context when read, because, while they all have their strengths, their weaknesses are that they do not tie the concepts together for a holistic approach to combat since they are all narrowly focused on one subject or another. Some are strong on strategy, forensics or philosophy but are lacking in combative principles or techniques. Some are almost all technique but lack the proper modality of training that can teach you to adapt. Attack Proof in our view bridges the gaps between these excellent works. Reading them will clarify in your mind why Grand Master Perkins *had to* create Guide Chaos.

Strong on Defense: Survival Rules to Protect You and Your Family from Crime, Sanford Strong, Atria (1996)

Arguably the scariest book on this list, this is the type of book that Grand Master Perkins himself has stated he wishes he had written. It is a collection of horrific violent acts perpetrated on ordinary people collected and assembled to shock you into reality. This book, while essential, is not for the feint of heart. It is graphic and pulls no punches.

Kill or Get Killed, Col Rex Applegate, Paladin Press, (1976)

This is an excellent book which explores not only the development of WWII combative skills but offers a variety of techniques which focus on taking bad guys out quickly. Do not be put off by some of the techniques that pertain to controlling or grappling type moves—remember, this book was also written for riot control and policing as a part of the US occupation forces in Japan and Europe after WWII.

The Close-Combat Files of Colonel Rex Applegate, Col Rex Applegate, Maj Chuck Melson, Paladin Press, (1998)

This is the story of how Col. Rex Applegate, William Fairbairn, Eric Sykes and Wild Bill Donovan trained and employed OSS and MID commandos during WWII. Many of these organizations were the forerunners of MI6, MI5, the SAS and the CIA. This book provides great historical context as to the development of some of the most effective fighting systems ever created. The simplicity and effectiveness of what they taught and the minimum training required for proficiency is eye-opening.

On Killing: The Psychological Cost of Learning to Kill in War and Society, Dave Grossman, Back Bay Books (1996)
Excellent book on the psychology of killing from an analytical perspective. While we don't agree with all of the author's conclusions it is an informative read nonetheless.

Go Rin No Sho (The Book of Five Rings) Miyamoto Musashi, Shambhala; New Ed edition (2005)
Shinmen Musashi No Kami Fujiwara No Genshin, or as he is commonly known, Miyamoto Musashi, was arguably the greatest swordsman to live during his time. It is recorded that he slew a man in single combat when he was just thirteen. He was the victor in over 60 duels and fought in six wars until he finally settled down at the age of 50. The Book of Five Rings is a classic and a primer for developing the proper Mushin Warrior mindset.

Sun Tzu, The Art of War, Ralph Sawyer, Westview Press; New Ed edition (1994) Probably one of the best books on military strategy and philosophy. These timeless principles are just as applicable today as when they were written over 2,000 years ago. Ralph Sawyer does a masterful job of providing the historical context to which the Art of War was written. When you read it (as with The Book of Five Rings) you will see the GC mindset principles throughout.

John Perkins
Grand Master

Grand Master John Perkins

- Grand Master in Combat Martial Arts under the International Combat Martial Arts Federation along with John McSweeny, Jeff Jarrett, Master Visitacion, and Col. Rex Applegate.
- Grand Master and Founder of Guided Chaos and Guided Chaos Combatives
- Named "America's Foremost Self Protection Expert" (Trends Research Institute)

Lt Col Al Ridenhour USMC

- Close Combat Master
- Former Anti Terrorism/Force Protection Officer for Multi-National Forces West in Iraq
- Counter Terror/Physical Security Expert
- Veteran Operation Iraqi Freedom
- Veteran Persian Gulf War

Al Ridenhour
7th Degree Master

John Perkins

- Former Yonkers, NY Detective.
- Forensic crime scene reconstruction expert.
- Police veteran of over 100 documented brutal arrests of extremely violent criminals, where people ended up in the hospital or morgue.
- Engaged in unlicensed Pit-fighting on the docks of Newark and New Orleans pre-UFC (no rules except for don't kill the other guy).
- One of the top Close Contact and Point Shooting instructors in the U.S.
- Student of Thomas Loughnan "The fastest man in the world" with a Colt 45 1911 semi-automatic.
- Holds the rank of Grand Master in Combat Martial Arts under the International Combat Martial Arts Federation along with John McSweeny, Jeff Jarrett, Master Visitacion, and Col. Rex Applegate.
- Bodyguard to Billionaire publisher Malcolm Forbes, Israeli Defense minister Moshe Dayan, EST founder Werner Ehrard; trained bodyguards to Pope John Paul II.
- Trained by his father from the age of 5 in World War II Close Quarters Combat and Native American Catch Wrestling; Combat Hapkido by Master Ik Jo Kang (instructor for the Korean ROK Army during the Vietnam War); Elephtheri Pali (Greek: "Ruthless Combat") by George Kaperonis and by Temple Trained Chicago Tai Chi Master Waysun Liao.
- In 1978, Perkins created Guided Chaos, a completely original system of self-defense that *adapts* to violent attacks.
- Author of best-selling self-defense books, used as training manuals for members of the U.S. Marines, U.S. Army, Royal Canadian Mounted Police, NYPD, the Guardian Angels Capetown South Africa chapter ("The Most Violent City in the World") and select Reality-based and kung fu schools around the globe.

--**Questions?** Email us at
http://attackproof.com/ASKATTACKPROOFFORM

--**Join a discussion** at http://attackproof.com/new-guided-chaos-self-defense-forum-entrance.html

--**Join a local informal Training Group** at
http://attackproof.com/INTERACT.html

42619953R00076

Made in the USA
Middletown, DE
16 April 2019